Communications in Computer and Information Science 1329

More information about this series at http://www.springer.com/series/7899

Huansheng Ning · Feifei Shi (Eds.)

Cyberspace Data and Intelligence, and Cyber-Living, Syndrome, and Health

International 2020 Cyberspace Congress, CyberDI/CyberLife 2020
Beijing, China, December 10–12, 2020
Proceedings

 Springer

Editors
Huansheng Ning 🆔
University of Science
and Technology Beijing
Beijing, China

Feifei Shi 🆔
University of Science
and Technology Beijing
Beijing, China

ISSN 1865-0929   ISSN 1865-0937   (electronic)
Communications in Computer and Information Science
ISBN 978-981-33-4335-1   ISBN 978-981-33-4336-8   (eBook)
https://doi.org/10.1007/978-981-33-4336-8

This Springer imprint is published by the registered company Springer Nature Singapore Pte Ltd.
The registered company address is: 152 Beach Road, #21-01/04 Gateway East, Singapore 189721, Singapore

Preface

The volume contains the papers from the 2020 Cyberspace Congress (CyberCon 2020) which includes the International Conference on Cyberspace Data and Intelligence (CyberDI 2020) and the International Conference on Cyber-Living, Cyber-Syndrome and Cyber-Health (CyberLife 2020) held online during December 10–12, 2020.

The recent advances in Smart IoT and Artificial Intelligence have driven cyberspace into a new prosperous era, and cyberspace in turn has expanded to novel and interesting domains such as Cyberspace Intelligence, Cyber-living, and Cyber-life. The brilliant CyberCon 2020 continues to explore the cutting-edge techniques related to hot topics in cyberspace, and it consists of CyberDI 2020 and CyberLife 2020. We sincerely welcome leading experts, researchers, and scholars in cyberspace, cyber-data, cyber-intelligence, cyber-living, and other emerging technologies attending the congress and serving as a guide to the state of the art.

To be honest, cyberspace has become the fourth space for human survival in addition to the traditional physical, social, and thinking spaces. It is attracting increasing attention, while meantime many issues and challenges need to be understood in depth. In CyberDI 2020 and CyberLife 2020, advanced theories, techniques, applications regarding data and intelligence, topics and researches about cyber-syndrome, cyber-health, and cyber-living are underlined and envisioned well. CyberDI 2020 mainly focused on intelligent ways of making full use of the data, depending on algorithms such as deep learning, neural networks and knowledge graph, and CyberLife 2020 concentrated on modern technologies like image processing or data science in Cyber-health systems.

In order to ensure the high quality of both conferences, we followed a rigorous review process in CyberDI 2020 and CyberLife 2020. The CyberDI 2020 and CyberLife 2020 received 36 qualified submissions in total, and 13 papers were accepted finally, most of which are full papers. All manuscripts were reviewed by at least three peer-reviewers with a single-blind review process, on the basis of their qualifications and experiences.

The proceedings editors wish to thank the dedicated conference committee members and all the other reviewers for their contributions. Sincerely, we hope these proceedings will help a lot for all interested readers. And we also thank Springer for their trust and for publishing the proceeding of the CyberDI 2020 and CyberLife 2020.

October 2020

Huansheng Ning
Feifei Shi

Organization

CyberDI 2020

General Chairs

Mahmoud Daneshmand	Stevens Institute of Technology, USA
Yinglong Xia	Facebook, USA

Program Committee Chairs

Jie He	University of Science and Technology Beijing, China
Kim-Kwang Raymond Choo	The University of Texas at San Antonio, USA
Ravi Sandhu	The University of Texas at San Antonio, USA

Steering Committee

Liming Chen	Ulster University, UK
Mahmoud Daneshmand	Stevens Institute of Technology, USA
Keping Long	University of Science and Technology Beijing, China
Huansheng Ning	University of Science and Technology Beijing, China
Chunming Rong	University of Stavanger, Norway

Program Committee

Farhan Ahmad	University of Derby, UK
Cuneyt Gurcan Akcora	University of Manitoba, Canada
Valerio Arnaboldi	IIT-CNR, Italy
Elisa Bertino	Purdue University, USA
Kaigui Bian	Peking University, China
Licia Capra	University College London, UK
Fu Chen	Central University of Finance and Economics, China
Sahraoui Dhelim	University of Science and Technology Beijing, China
Giancarlo Fortino	University of Calabria, Italy
Jin Guo	University of Science and Technology Beijing, China
Octavio Loyola-González	Tecnologico de Monterrey, Mexico
Guangjie Han	Hohai University, China
Jun Han	Swinburne University of Technology, Australia
Richard Hill	University of Huddersfield, UK
Fahim Kawsar	Bell Labs, Belgium
Robert Kaufman	The University of Texas at San Antonio, USA
Mike Chieh-Jan Liang	Microsoft Research, China
Huai Liu	Swinburne University of Technology, Australia
Kai Liu	Chongqing University, China

Qinghua Lu	CSIRO, Australia
Alessandra Mileo	National University of Ireland, Ireland
Changhai Nie	Nanjing University, China
Constantinos Patsakis	University of Piraeus, Greece
Siripen Pongpaichet	University of California Irvine, USA
Lianyong Qi	Qufu Normal University, China
Tie Qiu	Tianjin University, China
Stefanos Vrochidis	Information Technologies Institute, Greece
Shangguang Wang	Beijing University of Posts and Telecommunications, China
Xiang Wang	Beihang University, China
Matthew Williams	University of Birmingham, UK
Weiguang Wu	Sun Yat-sen University, China
Nicholas Yuan	Microsoft Research, China
Liqiang Zhang	Indiana University South Bend, USA
Qi Zhang	IBM T J Watson, USA
Yujun Zhang	Chinese Academy of Sciences, China
Chunsheng Zhu	Southern University of Science and Technology, China

CyberLife 2020

General Chairs

| Sajal K. Das | Missouri University of Science and Technology, USA |
| María Fernanda Cabrera Umpiérrez | Universidad Politécnica de Madrid, Spain |

Program Committee Chairs

| Diego López-de-Ipiña González-de-Artaza | Universidad de Deusto, Spain |
| Liming Chen | Ulster University, UK |

Steering Committee

Liming Chen	Ulster University, UK
Huansheng Ning	University of Science and Technology Beijing, China
Chunming Rong	University of Stavanger, Norway

Program Committee

Nasser Alaraje	Michigan Technological University, USA
Abbes Amira	De Montfort University, UK
Kofi Appiah	University of York, UK
Hussain Al-Aqrabi	University of Huddersfield, UK
Junaid Arshad	University of West London, UK
Maher Assaad	Ajman University, UAE
Muhammad Ajmal Azad	University of Derby, UK

Xingzhen Bai	Shandong University of Science and Technology, China
Faycal Bensaali	Qatar University, Qatar
Hamza Djelouat	Qatar University, Qatar
Zhengchao Dong	Columbia University, USA
Kieren Egan	University of Strathclyde, UK
Liangxiu Han	Manchester Metropolitan University, UK
Tan Jen Hong	National University of Singapore, Singapore
Yong Hu	The University of Hong Kong, China
Chenxi Huang	Xiamen University, China
Yizhang Jiang	Jiangnan University, China
Colin Johnson	University of Kent, UK
Jianxin Li	Beihang University, China
Yuexin Li	Hubei University, China
Ming Ma	University of Stanford, USA
Klaus D. McDonald-Maier	University of Essex, UK
Wajid Mumtaz	University of West Bohemia, Czech Republic
Raymond F. Muzic, jr	Case Western Reserve University, University Hospitals Cleveland Medical Center, USA
John Panneerselvam	University of Derby, UK
Preetha Phillips	West Virginia School of Osteopathic Medicine, USA
Pengjiang Qian	Jiangnan University, China
Rusdi Abd Rashid	University of Malaya Center for Addiction Sciences (UMCAS), Malaysia
Junding Sun	Henan Polytechnic University, China
Li Tan	Beijing Technology and Business University, China
Yanghong Tan	Hunan University, China
Liying Wang	Nanjing Normal University, China
Likun Xia	Capital Normal University, China
Kedi Xu	Zhejiang University, China
Xiaosong Yang	Bournemouth University, UK
Susu Yao	Institute for Infocomm Research, A*STAR, Singapore
Bin Ye	Queens University Belfast, UK
Jin Yong	Changshu Institute of Technology, China
Wangyang Yu	Shaanxi Normal University, China
Bo Yuan	University of Derby, UK
Xiaojun Zhai	University of Essex, UK
Da Zhang	Capital Normal University, China
Shaomin Zhang	Zhejiang University, China
Wenbing Zhao	Cleveland State University, USA
Yongjun Zheng	University of West London, UK
Shan Zhong	Changshu Institute of Technology, China
Zhifeng Zhong	Hubei University, China
Rongbo Zhu	South Central University for Nationalities, China

Contents

Machine Learning

Ubiquitous and Intelligent Computing

Machine Learning

Safety Supervision for Coal Mines Using Machine Learning Methods

Jun Zhang[1], Yunlong Wang[2,3,4], Dezhi Wang[5], Zhigang Zhao[2,3,4], and Xiong Luo[2,3,4]([⊠])

[1] Science and Technology Division, North China Institute of Science and Technology, Beijing 065201, China
[2] School of Computer and Communication Engineering, University of Science and Technology Beijing, Beijing 100083, China
xluo@ustb.edu.cn
[3] Beijing Key Laboratory of Knowledge Engineering for Materials Science, Beijing 100083, China
[4] Shunde Graduate School, University of Science and Technology Beijing, Foshan 528399, China
[5] School of Computer Science, North China Institute of Science and Technology, Beijing 065201, China

Abstract. Coals are of great importance to economic development, but the safety problem always affects the efficient production of coal mines. Then, safety supervision is the basis for guaranteeing the productive efficiency of coal mines. The safety supervisions were previously based on handcrafted models of reality. Nowadays, they are able to be achieved using data-driven learning approaches. Hence, to improve the supervision performance in consideration of complex characteristics of coal mine production data, this paper presents a machine learning scheme towards safety supervision. Generally speaking, there are two parts in the developed scheme. On the basis of bidirectional encoder representations from transformers (BERT) model, a regression prediction is firstly used to analyze the coal mine data, with the purpose of finding those possible accident attributions. Meanwhile, to tackle the issues of discovering the relationship in data, the unsupervised Apriori learning algorithm is also developed to mine these association rules in coal mine data. The presented scheme, named machine learning-based safe supervision (MLSS), is experimentally validated by using actual data collected from some coal mines in China. The results demonstrate that our method can achieve satisfactory analysis performance.

Keywords: Machine learning · Regression prediction · Apriori learning algorithm · Coal mine

1 Introduction

In consideration of its industrial particularity, coal mine production may have certain risks. During the production process, there are many dangerous elements and different

H. Ning and F. Shi (Eds.): CyberDI 2020/CyberLife 2020, CCIS 1329, pp. 3–14, 2020.
https://doi.org/10.1007/978-981-33-4336-8_1

risk factors in the coal mines, and many factors may lead to accidents. Safety supervision as a key in guaranteeing industrial production is to carry out investigation and analysis on the production process to find out and eliminate the hidden dangers of accidents for preventing them in the early stages. Through the use of safety supervision, the production automation of coal mines would be advanced, thus reducing hidden dangers and ensuring the improvement of workers' health level and life safety [1]. Meanwhile, some complex characteristics exist in the safety supervision data of coal mines. Specifically, due to the long production period of coal mines, the data of accident hidden checking records and risk control records are updated continuously, which makes the data processing and analysis more complicated. Therefore, there remain some technical challenges that should be addressed to achieve safety supervision.

In previous industrial production, the coal mine safety supervision was based on handcrafted models of reality, and it may be inefficient considering the application environment with large-scale coal mine data [2]. However, nowadays, they can be achieved using data-driven learning approaches. That is, after collecting safety supervision data in coal mines, some valuable information could be extracted and then fully exploited via machine learning methods.

Appropriate data mining technologies can improve production effectiveness while overcoming the limitations of mere manual operations. When the data mining algorithm is designed, it can achieve the automatic collation and analysis of data without manual intervention. Hence, through the analysis of the safety supervision data by using data mining technologies, we can obtain valuable information and predict and prevent safety accidents.

Among the machine learning methods for natural language processing (NLP) and information mining, bidirectional encoder representations from transformers (BERT) and Apriori are the practically resultful algorithms. Compared with other text analysis methods, BERT enables model pre-training on a large scale of data and then fine-tuning the model on the specific tasks. In addition, the deeper network structure is another important factor for the better performance of BERT. For association rule extraction, Apriori enables rule generation based on itemsets, and association relationships can be extracted automatically via Apriori, which saves plenty of resources compared with manual operation. Considering that the complex characteristics of coal mine production data impose a challenging obstacle to the safety supervision approach design problem, motivated by the BERT model and the unsupervised Apriori learning algorithm, a machine learning scheme towards regression prediction and rule mining on safety supervision data is developed in this paper, avoiding the limitations of those current safety supervision methods for coal mines and further improving the supervision performance.

Here, the contributions of this paper can be summarized as follows.

1) Aiming at the practical demand of safety supervision for coal mine production, a scheme named machine learning-based safe supervision (MLSS) is accordingly presented, which effectively improves the analysis performance of coal mine data.
2) In the field of coal mine safety supervision data analysis, through the use of BERT-based regression prediction model and Apriori learning algorithm, the developed scheme can find valuable information to exploit the potential of those coal mine data.

The rest of this paper is organized with the following way. Section 2 introduces the background, focusing on BERT model and Apriori algorithm. Additionally, Sect. 3 provides a description on the developed scheme. Then, Sect. 4 presents the experimental results on coal mine safety supervision data analysis to evaluate the performance of our scheme. Finally, the conclusion is given in Sect. 5.

2 Background

BERT, as a deep bidirectional encoder, has great potential to represent unlabeled text in coal mine safety supervision. Then, Apriori can extract the associated rules automatically in coal mine accidents for assistant decision-making by combining the attributes from BERT representation and original safety supervision data. Here, BERT and Apriori are introduced in this section firstly, and recent literature on coal mine safety using machine learning techniques is reviewed comprehensively in the following section.

2.1 BERT

For the safety production supervision data in coal mines, there are massive unlabeled texts. Then, a language representation model is necessary to achieve the data analysis task for safety supervision using machine learning methods. Unlike some other traditional NLP algorithms, BERT is a bidirectional transformer used in NN model, which is specifically designed to obtain deep bidirectional representations from unlabeled texts, and it has been successfully in a wide variety of NLP with state-of-the-art performance in recent years [3].

Generally, BERT has some layers; and there are a multi-head attention and a linear affine with the residual connection in each layer. A typical structure of BERT is shown in Fig. 1, where E_i and $T_i (i = 1, 2, \ldots, N)$ are the input and output vectors in this model, respectively. In Fig. 1, "Transformer" module is implemented using multi-head attention mechanism as follows [3, 4].

$$\text{Attention}(\mathbf{Q}, \mathbf{K}, \mathbf{V}) = \text{Softmax}\left(\frac{\mathbf{Q}\mathbf{K}^{\mathrm{T}}}{\sqrt{d_k}}\right)\mathbf{V}, \tag{1}$$

$$\text{head}_i(\mathbf{Q}, \mathbf{K}, \mathbf{V}) = \text{Attention}\left(\mathbf{Q}\mathbf{W}_i^{\mathbf{Q}}, \mathbf{K}\mathbf{W}_i^{\mathbf{K}}, \mathbf{V}\mathbf{W}_i^{\mathbf{V}}\right), \tag{2}$$

$$\text{MultiHead}(\mathbf{Q}, \mathbf{K}, \mathbf{V}) = \text{Concat}(\text{head}_1, \text{head}_2, \ldots, \text{head}_h)\mathbf{W}^{\mathbf{O}}, \tag{3}$$

where $\mathbf{Q}$, $\mathbf{K}$, and $\mathbf{V}$ are the query matrix, key matrix, and value matrix, respectively. Moreover, d_k is the dimension of $\mathbf{K}$, and $\mathbf{W}_i^{\mathbf{Q}}$, $\mathbf{W}_i^{\mathbf{K}}$, $\mathbf{W}_i^{\mathbf{V}}$, and $\mathbf{W}^{\mathbf{O}}$ are the parameter matrices. Here, (1) is designed for a single input query in the above multi-head attention mechanism, and the output can be computed in (3) by concatenating head$_i$ defined by (2).

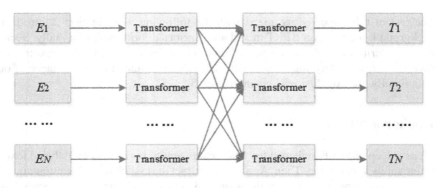

Fig. 1. A typical structure of BERT.

2.2 Apriori

Apriori algorithm, as a classical algorithm in association rule mining, can be used to find patterns for these frequent datasets, while providing an assistant in making some decisions [5, 6].

Let the implication of $A \rightarrow B$ be the association rule, where A and B are subsets of itemset and $A \cap B = \varnothing$. In addition, let $P(A \cap B)$ be the probability of an itemset containing set A and set B, and it is the "Support" defined as support$(A \rightarrow B)$. Moreover, let count$(\cdot)$ be the count of the itemset, and then "confidence" can be represented as confidence$(A \rightarrow B) = ($support$(A \cap B))/($support$(A)) = ($count$(A \cap B))/($count$(A))$.

Then, if Lift$(A \rightarrow B) = ($count$(A \cap B))/($count(A)count$(B)) > 1$, the $A \rightarrow B$ is a strong association rule. Meanwhile, if Lift$(A \rightarrow B) < 1$, the $A \rightarrow B$ is an invalid strong association rule, and if Lift$(A \rightarrow B) = 1$, the A and B are independent.

2.3 Coal Mine Safety Based on Machine Learning

With the rapid development of machine learning techniques, some machine learning algorithms have been used in the coal mine management system, including neural network (NN), genetic algorithm (GA), decision tree model, and some others [7]. The early warning of coal mine safety production was implemented using a back propagation (BP) NN with a fast convergence speed and a high precision [8]. Aiming at the characteristics of truck working condition data, predicting the safety status of coal mine trucks was achieved using recurrent neural network (RNN) [9]. Through the combination of self-organizing data mining (SODM) model and phase space reconstruction (PSR) technique, a prediction model was proposed to analyze the time-series data generated in complex systems of gas emission in coal mines [10]. In [11], after analyzing hidden hazard data in the coal mines, the data mining was conducted on four dimensions, i.e., department, category, level, and address of hidden hazard. Then, the assistant decision-making was given while providing strong association rules among the above four dimensions. In [12], for the data collected by wireless sensor networks in the coal mine monitoring and prewarning system, a data aggregation strategy and fuzzy assessment-based prewarning model were proposed to prevent the possible accidents.

Furthermore, in addition to the above works, some other requirements, e.g., accident classification and prediction, rule mining, are also achieved by using the machine learning methods. As far as the issue of classification, there are some advancements. For examples, after collecting the data of coal mine disasters from 2000 to 2016 in China and sorting them, through the analysis in accordance with features, e.g., time, region, and type, the possible classification rules of major coal mine accidents were analyzed, and some corresponding suggestions were accordingly presented [13]. For the experimental area with the size of 1000×1000 pixels in Hegang coal mining area, the NN and support vector machine (SVM) classification methods were used to classify land use in coal mining area [14]. The coal mine safety investment influence factors were discussed, and then the coal mine safety investment prediction model was developed using SVM. After comparing with the traditional BP network approach via experiments, the feasibility and effectivity of the proposed model were verified [15]. A decision classification model was proposed to predict the injury situations via the information and data concerned while serving the purpose of guiding the safety management of such accidents [16]. For the risk assessment task used to revise coal mine regulations, a Bayesian network-based method of quantitatively assessing the risk of gas explosion in coal mines was proposed. Then, the potential causes of accidents could be determined [17].

Additionally, for the rule mining of coal mine safety data, there are also some works recently. After preprocessing the safety hidden danger data of coal mine workplaces, those valuable association rules inside the data were extracted using an improved Apriori algorithm [18]. Furthermore, in [19], the ontology technology was used to organize coal mine safety monitor data, and the association rule was developed to mine the mass monitoring data while achieving the hidden reasoning rules for the early-warning task. In a coal mine safety monitoring system, the correlation analysis algorithms Apriori and FP-growth were applied to design a model for coal mine gas monitoring, improving the performance of coal mine gas safety monitoring and early warning [20]. To improve rule mining algorithm used in the field of coal mine safety supervision, some optimization strategies and machine learning models are also incorporated into this method. For example, the improved fruit fly optimization algorithm (IFOA) and the general regression NN model were combined to model the coal and gas outburst prediction situations, and the sensitivity analysis was implemented to find the sensitive factors of coal and gas outbursts. Moreover, an Apriori algorithm was employed to mine the disaster information [21]. For the works mentioned above, although some valuable rules are obtained, the preprocessing operation is simple, and then the analysis performance could be further improved.

3 The Developed Machine Learning Scheme

There are two parts in the developed machine learning scheme MLSS, including the BERT-based regression prediction model and Apriori-based rule extraction algorithm. Such framework of the scheme MLSS is in Fig. 2. Then, we present the implementation processes of those parts.

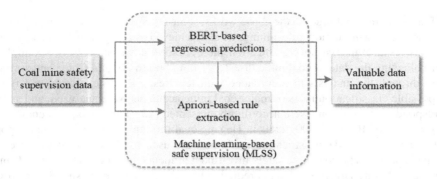

Fig. 2. The framework of MLSS.

3.1 The BERT-Based Regression Prediction

BERT, as an advanced pre-trained model, achieves popularity as soon as it was proposed. In this article, to achieve better performance on accident regression prediction, a trained BERT is transferred to encode the input attributions to numeric vectors. Then, the numeric vectors are feed into a logistic model to fit the relation between input attributions and output risk values. On the whole, three core steps can be concluded in this regression prediction.

Step 1: Encode text attributions into sentence vectors.

There are k attributes for each sample of coal mine safety supervision, including risk and its consequences description, type, and some others.

After inputting the above i-th attribution into BERT model, we can obtain a l-dimension sentence vector $\mathbf{w}_i = (v_1, v_2, \ldots, v_l)(i = 1, 2, \ldots, k)$. Then, the sample is accordingly represented as:

$$x = \sum_{i=1}^{k} \mathbf{w}_i. \tag{4}$$

Step 2: Train a logistic regression model.

Supposing y be the accident risk value of sample x, after being trained by a widely used stochastic gradient descent algorithm, the relation between input attributions and output risk values can be established according to the following formulas:

$$z = rx + b, \tag{5}$$

$$y = \frac{1}{1 + \exp(-z)}, \tag{6}$$

Step 3: Output the predicted values of the data in the test set.

In the test phase, the sample values of the data in the test set are computed by (4) firstly. Then the predicted risk values, including risk occurrence possibility, predicted accident loss and predicted accident severity, are obtained according to (5) and (6).

3.2 The Apriori-Based Rule Extraction

Here, we analyze the "Risk factors" and "Risk and consequence description" attributes in the coal mine safety supervision data, and mine the association rules via Apriori algorithm.

In the implementation, we should extract the corresponding keywords from antecedent and consequent, and the single use of text segmentation function could not achieve satisfactory performance. Hence, after labeling the keywords from the text artificially, we extract the keywords through the use of Jieba tool [22].

With the extracted keywords from the "Risk factors" and "Risk and consequence description" attributes, we can mine the association rules. Let K_1 and K_2 be the keywords set of "Risk factors" and "Risk and consequence description" attributes respectively, $A \in K_1$ and $B \in K_2$, "Items" be a set containing all samples, "Item(A)" denotes the set in which those samples contain set A, and then the "Support" of set A is defined as:

$$support(A) = \frac{count(Item(A))}{count(Items)}. \tag{7}$$

Meanwhile, the "confidence" of rule "$A \to B$" is represented as:

$$confidence(A \to B) = \frac{support(A \cap B)}{support(A)}. \tag{8}$$

The association rule "$A \to B$" can be extracted according to (7) and (8). After further sorting the rules from high to low by the confidence values, the final credible association rules are output.

It should be noted here that, when directly using Apriori algorithm, the fact may be inconsistent with the derived association rule "$A \to B$" in some cases. Then, the causal relationship may be inverted. Therefore, the Apriori algorithm is accordingly improved while adding the causal relationship coercively.

4 Experiment and Analysis

The experimental results and some discussions are provided in this section.

4.1 Experimental Description

In our experiment, 1734 data samples on the coal mine safety supervision are from a real coal mine in China. Taking the whole process into consideration, the data is from 8 units which are easy to appear safety problems in the actual production process, including Teams, Fully-mechanized coal mining, Routine inspection risk issues, Tunneling, Mechanical conveying, Ventilation and fire prevention, Civil engineering, and Boiler room. Each of the data is a safety supervision record consisting of 6 attributions, i.e., Risk factors, Risk and consequence description, Possibility (P), Risk value (D), Management criteria, and Management measures. The data statistics are summarized in Table 1.

Table 1. The experimental dataset.

Unit	The # of data samples
Teams	214
Fully-mechanized coal mining	224
Routine inspection risk issues	55
Tunneling	396
Mechanical conveying	347
Ventilation and fire prevention	410
Civil engineering	54
Boiler room	34

In the experiment, the data are randomly divided into training set and test set with the ratio 9:1, and the scheme is trained on the training set, and then the predicted value is estimated on the test set.

Specifically, the performance of regression prediction in this experiment is tested through the metric mean squared error (MSE) as follows.

$$\text{MSE} = \frac{1}{n} \sum_{i=1}^{n} \left(q_i - \hat{q}_i \right)^2, \tag{9}$$

where n is the number of samples, q_i is the labeled value for the i-th sample, and $\hat{q}_i$ is the predicted value for the i-th sample using the developed scheme.

Furthermore, the coefficient of determination (R^2) is also evaluated, and it is defined by:

$$R^2 = 1 - \frac{\sum_{i=1}^{n-1} \left(q_i - \hat{q}_i \right)^2}{\sum_{i=1}^{n-1} \left(q_i - \bar{q}_i \right)^2}, \tag{10}$$

where $\bar{q}_i$ is the average value for the labeled value q_i.

4.2 Experimental Results

In the training data, three indicators, i.e., the occurrence possibility of this accident (Possibility), the estimated losses due to this accident (Loss) and severity of this accident (Seriousness), are scored by the expertise in accordance with the corresponding production environment in the record. Here, in this experiment, we conduct the BERT-based regression analysis on this mine safety supervision data to predict the three indicators. Then, the MSE and the R^2 based on the scores from the expertise and our predicted results based on machine learning are achieved in Tables 2 and 3, respectively.

In Table 2, it is shown that the closer the MSE is to 0, the better the fitting result is. Meanwhile, the closer the coefficient of determination is to 1, the better the predicted results are. From Table 3, we can find that satisfactory performance is achieved using

Table 2. The MSE using the BERT-based regression prediction.

MSE	Possibility	Loss	Seriousness
Teams	1.13	0.65	–
Fully-mechanized coal mining	0.03	0.03	–
Routine inspection risk issues	0.48	–	0.62
Tunneling	1.23	0.98	–
Mechanical conveying	1.61	–	0.93
Ventilation and fire prevention	2.58	–	0.62
Civil engineering	0.21	–	1.37
Boiler room	0.51	–	0.93

Table 3. The coefficient of determination (R^2) using the BERT-based regression prediction.

R^2	Possibility	Loss	Seriousness
Teams	0.55	0.54	–
Fully-mechanized coal mining	0.83	0.91	–
Routine inspection risk issues	0.59	–	0.63
Tunneling	0.06	0.49	–
Mechanical conveying	−0.34	–	0.42
Ventilation and fire prevention	−1.86	–	0.74
Civil engineering	0.76	–	−0.21
Boiler room	−0.02	–	−0.35

the BERT-based regression prediction model. Through the prediction and analysis of the possibility, loss, and seriousness, it enables us to predict and prevent accidents in coal mines effectively.

On the other hand, the Apriori-based extraction algorithm is developed to mine the association rules from "Risk factors" and "Risk and consequence description" attributes. Since there are different data volumes at different working locations in the experimental data, the extracted rules are more effective when a larger dataset is available. In Table 4, we provide three extracted association rules with the top three value "confidence", while applying Apriori algorithm in "Mechanical conveying" and "Ventilation and fire prevention" unit samples.

From Table 4, we can observe that in mechanical conveying space, the failure to lock as required would easily lead to equipment misoperation and miscarriage of electricity. Additionally, in ventilation and fire prevention space, the failure to inspect as required would result in personnel injuries, and the seal quality dissatisfying regulations may lead to gas combustion and hypoxia and asphyxia. Through the rule mining for the data

Table 4. The association rules in units mechanical conveying and ventilation and fire prevention.

Unit	Association rule	Support	Confidence
Mechanical conveying	"Failure to lock as required" → "Equipment misoperation"	0.032	1.000
	"Failure to lock as required, Power failure" → "Miscarriage of electricity"	0.032	1.000
	"Failure to lock as required, Power failure" → "Equipment misoperation, Miscarriage of electricity"	0.032	1.000
Ventilation and fire prevention	"Failure to inspect as required" → "Personnel injuries"	0.015	0.600
	"Seal quality dissatisfying regulations" → "Gas combustion or explosion"	0.010	1.000
	"Seal quality dissatisfying regulations" → "Hypoxia and asphyxia"	0.010	1.000

in mechanical conveying and ventilation and fire prevention spaces, we can achieve the high confidence accident causality, and then the accidents would be prevented or predicted in advance.

5 Conclusion

This paper aims at addressing an important issue in the design of methods used to coal mine safety supervision. Motivated by some advanced machine learning models, a scheme MLSS mainly combining BERT and Apriori, is developed to improve the supervision performance. In the MLSS, the BERT-based regression prediction algorithm is used to analyze the coal mine safety supervision data, while predicting the possibility of risk occurrence and the loss. It is, therefore, expected that the risk factors with higher possibility and greater loss could be easily found. Then, the early-prevention is accordingly achieved. Moreover, we mine and analyze the risk factors and results in mechanical conveying and ventilation and fire prevention spaces, so that the association rules with strong causality are obtained. It enables different operation units to estimate the danger according to their situation and to prevent the occurrence of accidents. The proposed scheme provides a new direction on the research on coal mine safety supervision by combining pre-trained techniques and association rule mining methods. In future research, exploring the way to feed the associate rules into the regression prediction for model adaptation is the focus point.

Acknowledgement. This work was supported in part by the National Key Research and Development Program of China under Grant 2018YFC0808306, by the Scientific and Technological Innovation Foundation of Shunde Graduate School, USTB, under Grant BK19BF006, and by the Fundamental Research Funds for the University of Science and Technology Beijing under Grant FRF-BD-19-012A.

References

1. Xu, H., Fan, G.: Design of safety production supervision and data management system based on cloud platform. In: Abawajy, J.H., Choo, K.-K.R., Islam, R., Xu, Z., Atiquzzaman, M. (eds.) ATCI 2019. AISC, vol. 1017, pp. 584–591. Springer, Cham (2020). https://doi.org/10.1007/978-3-030-25128-4_72
2. Zhao, Z., Wei, Y., Wang, X., Li, R., Deng, J.: Efficient hidden danger prediction for safety supervision system: an advanced neural network learning method. In: Deng, Z. (ed.) CIAC 2017. LNEE, vol. 458, pp. 465–472. Springer, Singapore (2018). https://doi.org/10.1007/978-981-10-6445-6_51
3. Devlin, J., Chang, M.W., Lee, K., Toutanova, K.: BERT: pre-training of deep bidirectional transformers for language understanding. In: The Conference of the North American Chapter of the Association for Computational Linguistics: Human Language Technologies, Minneapolis, pp. 4171–4186. Association for Computational Linguistics (2019)
4. Vaswani, A., et al.: Attention is all you need. In: The 31st Annual Conference on Neural Information Processing Systems, Long Beach, CA, pp. 5999–6009. Neural Information Processing Systems Foundation (2017)
5. Agrawal, R., Srikant, R.: Fast algorithms for mining association rules in large databases. In: The 20th International Conference on Very Large Data Bases, San Mateo, CA, pp. 487–499. Morgan Kaufmann (1994)
6. Luna, J.M., Padillo, F., Pechenizkiy, M., Ventura, S.: Apriori versions based on mapreduce for mining frequent patterns on big data. IEEE Trans. Cybern. **48**(10), 2851–2865 (2018)
7. Qiao, W., Liu, Q., Li, X., Luo, X., Wan, Y.: Using data mining techniques to analyze the influencing factor of unsafe behaviors in Chinese underground coal mines. Resour. Policy **59**, 210–216 (2018)
8. Wang, Y., Lu, C., Zuo, C.: Coal mine safety production forewarning based on improved BP neural network. Int. J. Min. Sci. Technol. **25**(2), 319–324 (2015)
9. Fan, Y., Erdemutu, E., Jiao, X., Mo, X.: Mine-used truck working condition monitoring system based on data mining for Zhungeer energy open-pit. Saf. Coal Mines **50**(6), 146–148 (2019)
10. Li, R., Wu, Y., Shi, S., Zhu, H.: Research on self-organizing data mining method for time series prediction of gas emission in coal mine. J. Saf. Sci. Technol. **13**(7), 18–23 (2017)
11. Chen, Y.: Application of data mining technology in coal mine hidden hazard management. Ind. Mine Autom. **42**(2), 27–30 (2016)
12. Xia, X., Chen, Z., Wei, W.: Research on monitoring and prewarning system of accident in the coal mine based on big data. Sci. Program. **2018**, 9308742 (2018)
13. Zhu, Y., Wang, D., Li, D., Qi, X., Shao, Z.: Statistics analysis of serious coal mine disasters from 2000 to 2016 in China. China Energy Environ. Prot. **40**(9), 40–43 (2018)
14. Wang, L., Jia, Y., Yao, Y., Xu, D.: Accuray assessment of land use classification using support vector machine and neural network for coal mining area of Hegang city. China. Nat. Environ. Pollut. Technol. **18**(1), 335–341 (2019)
15. Chen, X., Cai, W., Chen, N.: Coal mine safety investment prediction based on support vector machine. In: The 5th International Conference on Natural Computation, Tianjian, pp. 199–202. IEEE (2009)

16. Lin, Y.: Analysis and prediction of injury severity of coal mine accidents based on decision tree. J. Saf. Envir. **17**(2), 591–596 (2017)
17. Li, M., Wang, H., Wang, D., Shao, Z., He, S.: Risk assessment of gas explosion in coal mines based on fuzzy AHP and Bayesian network. Process Saf. Environ. Prot. **135**, 207–218 (2020)
18. Liu, S., Peng, L.: Analysis of coal mine hidden danger correlation based on improved apriori algorithm. In: The 4th International Conference on Intelligent Systems Design and Engineering Applications, Zhangjiajie, pp. 112–116. IEEE (2013)
19. Wand, X., Zhu, J., Meng, X., He, Y.: A model of safety monitoring and early warning for coal mine based on ontology and association rules. Min. Saf. Environ. Prot. **46**(3), 27–31 (2019)
20. Shi, J., Shi, J.: Application of correlation analysis on data mining in coal mine gas safety monitoring and early warning. China Energy Environ. Prot. **39**(8), 1–5 (2017)
21. Xie, X., et al.: Risk prediction and factors risk analysis based on IFOA-GRNN and apriori algorithms: application of artificial intelligence in accident prevention. Process Saf. Environ. Prot. **122**, 169–184 (2019)
22. Jieba Chinese text segmentation. https://github.com/fxsjy/jieba. Accessed 1 Aug 2020

Iterative Optimization for Edge Federated Learning

Shilong Chai[1], Mu Gu[2], Jiehan Zhou[3(✉)], Weishan Zhang[4], and Xingjie Zeng[4]

[1] Technical University of Darmstadt, Darmstadt, Germany
shilong92.chai@gmail.com
[2] Beijing Aerospace Smart Manufacturing Technology Development Co., Ltd.,
Beijing, China
[3] University of Oulu, Oulu, Finland
jiehan.zhou@gmail.com
[4] China University of Petroleum, Qingdao, China

Abstract. Federated learning emphasizes the protection of data privacy in distributed machine learning. It is similar to the data-centered distributed machine learning that trains a model for making predictions or decisions without being explicitly programmed. The computing workers in federated learning provide training for the model at the edges of network where the data are stored. Thus, they can control the data and decide whether and when participating in the learning is needed. This paper analyzes the difference between centralized machine learning and federated learning, and the affects of communication frequency between the server and clients on the learning accuracy. It proposes two variations of federated learning optimizations by studying its process. The experimental results demonstrate that the centralized machine learning often receives a far better training result under the same number of training samples compared with federated learning. Furthermore, increasing the communication frequency between the server and clients can improve the learning result.

Keywords: Federated learning · Distributed machine learning · Data privacy · Communication frequency · Variations · Result improvement

1 Introduction

The integration of Internet of Things with cloud computing presents emerging challenges and chances for unmanned driving [1,2], intelligent transportation [3], equipment optimization [4], process optimization[5], full factory value chain optimization [6], and virtual factories [7]. However, data-centralized processing presents the following defects.

1. Data delay: transmitting data to the cloud for training may cause queuing and propagation network latency, and it is often impossible to meet real-time scenarios;

© Springer Nature Singapore Pte Ltd. 2020
H. Ning and F. Shi (Eds.): CyberDI 2020/CyberLife 2020, CCIS 1329, pp. 15–26, 2020.
https://doi.org/10.1007/978-981-33-4336-8_2

2. Privacy disclosure: transmitting data to the cloud center may cause privacy concerns from users who own the data.

In order to solve the above issues, Edge Federated Learning has attracted extensive attention [8,9]. Edge Computing provides users with services by forming a unified computing platform with network and storage on the network edge, so that data can be processed and trained in a timely and effective manner near the data source. **Federated learning (FL)** in the edge presents a feasible solution that meets privacy protection and data security, which is driven by the following application scenarios.

Scaling up deep learning leads to distributed learning: the increasing scale of deep learning can dramatically improve the performance of deep neural networks [10,11]. As a result, distributed learning is being emerged where multiple machines are used for model optimization. Although many state-of-the-art distributed learning algorithms have achieved the distributed characteristic through assigning the computation task to several computing nodes, the computation locations are still centralized. In addition, from the data perspective, they have to be collected to the data center. Sending data to the data center can cause privacy problems as well.

Demand for Information Privacy Protection: It has become a worldwide trend to value data privacy and security. Every leak of public data attracts significant attention from the media and the public. Therefore, countries are strengthening the protection of data security and privacy. The USA enacted the Consumer Privacy Bill of Rights in 2012 [12], the EU introduced GDPR (General Data Protection Regulation) in 2016 [13], and China commenced the Cybersecurity Law of the People's Republic of China in 2017 [14]. Increasingly strict user data privacy and security management have brought an unprecedented challenge for data collection.

This paper aims to study the difference between data-centered distributed machine learning and edge federated learning, and further understand the effectiveness of edge federated learning. The contribution to this paper is as follows:

1. to compare the convergence rate between federated learning where training data distribute across clients, model is trained on clients locally and centralized aggregated, and conventional centralized machine learning where all training data are collected to a data center, then applied to train mode, with the same amount of training data.
2. to develop two variants of federated learning, they are termed as epoch-wise federated learning and batch-wise federated learning. Since every update by the client can be seen as an incremental improvement shared to the current received model, and the current model is an integration of improvements acorss all clients from the beginning to the current learning state. These three different federated learning methods would be used to determine, if the convergence rate will be increased when the clients share their improvements more frequently.

The remainder of the paper is organized as follows. Section 1 introduces federated learning; Sect. 2 designs two optimization variants of federated learning based on communication frequency; Sect. 3 presents the experiment; and Sect. 3.3 evaluates the results; Sect. 4 summarizes the paper.

2 Federated Learning

Conventional machine learning algorithms require centralizing the training data on a machine or in a data center. As mobile phones and tablets have become primary computing devices for many people, federated learning enables model training by utilizing the cheap computation available at the edges of the network since the local datasets at the edges are also restricted [11,15]. A prediction model is collaboratively trained by a set of mobile devices in federated learning instead of on a data center conventionally.

2.1 Federated Learning Process

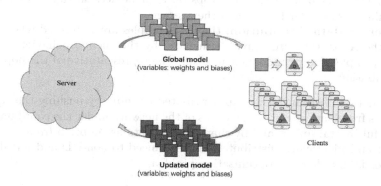

Fig. 1. A typical federated learning process

A typical federated learning process is illustrated in Fig. 1:

1. Client selection: Practical federated learning scenarios usually involve hundreds of thousands of mobile devices, but without all in use, and it is not necessary to include all client devices for every simple iteration. The server selects only a subset of clients for collaboratively training a shared prediction model.
2. Model broadcasting: The server broadcasts the current global model parameters to the selected clients.
3. Model training: Each selected client device trains the model using their local data, and eventually generates an update to the current model parameters.
4. Updates aggregation: The server aggregates the updates from all selected client devices.
5. Model Update: The model parameters are updated based on the updates from clients.

2.2   Federated Optimization

The optimization problem in federated learning is referred to as federated optimization. The goal of federated learning is to find a proper set of parameters constructing the neural network that minimizes the loss function over the whole training dataset consisting of the individual training datasets of all training-participating clients. This learning seems similar to distributed learning. The difference for optimization might be the characteristics of federated learning, they also describe some of the challenges in federated learning as follows.

- **Massively distributed:** The computing nodes of federated learning are the edge devices like mobile phones or tablets, which are frequently carried along by people who are distributed and move in a wide area.
- **A huge number of clients:** In federated learning scenarios, computing nodes are the client's device; usually, millions of clients are involved in the learning.
- **An unbalanced number of training samples:** some users might more frequently use some services or Apps on their devices so that they generate training datasets far larger than the average.
- **Different data distribution:** the data samples are generated when clients use the Apps, they are heavily influenced by the client's behavior. A single data sample of any random client cannot be representative of the population distribution.

Thus, federated learning scales up distributed learning by pushing the computing nodes from data center to the edges of the network under the coordination of a powerful central server, and by changing the data assumption from IID (Independent and Identically Distributed) and balanced to non-IID and unbalanced, which leads to a different optimization problem.

2.3   The Federated Averaging Algorithm

A federated optimization algorithm named Federated Averaging (FedAvg) is proposed in [11]. When FedAvg is performed, at first the server broadcasts the global model parameters to the training participants, each client is allowed to perform mini-batch gradient descent algorithm to optimize the model several times, each time with a single mini-batch.

FedAvg performs federated learning as described previously. A small change is, the training-participated clients send the updated model parameters (weights and biases) as updates rather than the gradients back to server. The assumption behind FedAvg is that the global model parameters received by clients in each round are identical, and averaging the gradients is equivalent to averaging the parameters themselves. Assume K clients participate in the training, the gradient computed by client k on its local data at the current model parameters $\mathbf{w}_t$ is g_k, then the central server aggregates these gradients and uses them to update the global model parameters:

$$\mathbf{w}_{t+1} = \mathbf{w}_t - \eta \sum_{k=1}^{K} \frac{n_k}{N} g_k \qquad (1)$$

where η is the learning rate, N is the number of the entire training samples across all training-participated clients in the round, n_k is the number of the training samples of client k. That is equivalent to

$$\begin{aligned}
\mathbf{w}_{t+1} &= \frac{n_1}{N}(\mathbf{w}_t - \eta g_1) + \frac{n_2}{N}(\mathbf{w}_t - \eta g_2) + ... + \frac{n_K}{N}(\mathbf{w}_t - \eta g_K) \\
&= \frac{n_1}{N}(\mathbf{w}_{t+1}^1) + \frac{n_2}{N}(\mathbf{w}_{t+1}^2) + ... + \frac{n_K}{N}(\mathbf{w}_{t+1}^K) \\
&= \sum_{k=1}^{K} \frac{n_k}{N}\mathbf{w}_{t+1}^k
\end{aligned} \qquad (2)$$

where $\mathbf{w}_{t+1}$ is the updated global model parameters, $\mathbf{w}_{t+1}^k$ is the updated model parameters of client k.

The complete pseudo-code is given in Algorithm 1.

Algorithm 1. Federated Averaging

Server executes:
initialize $\mathbf{w}_0$
for each round $t = 1,2,...$**do**
$S_t =$ (random set of K clients)
for each client $k \in S_t$ **in parallel do**
$\mathbf{w}_{t+1}^k \Leftarrow$ ClientUpdate $(k, \mathbf{w}_t)$
$\mathbf{w}_{t+1} \Leftarrow \sum_{k=1}^{N} \frac{n_k}{N}\mathbf{w}_{t+1}^k$

ClientUpdate(k,w): for client $k = 1,2,...,K$ **do**
$\mathbf{w}_{t+1}^k \Leftarrow \mathbf{w}_t^k - \eta g_k$
return $\mathbf{w}_{t+1}^k$ to server

- **Batch size:** it is the number of training samples on forward/backward pass. In gradient descent algorithm, the full dataset is used to calculated the loss function, but realistically it is impossible or costly. Therefore, the mini-batch gradient descent is in use, where an estimate of the full dataset (known as batch) is used to calculate the loss function for a single iteration. For instance, the dataset contains 2000 training samples, and is often equally divided into 40 partitions, each partition consists of 50 training samples, and the number of 50 is the batch size.
- **Epoch:** an epoch refers to one cycle through the full training dataset. In the given instance, if all 2000 training samples are fed into a neural network, or in other words, if all batches with batch size 50 are fed into the neural network (40 steps in total), that is called one epoch.

- **Iteration:** iteration is the number of batches required to complete one epoch. Again in the given instance, the number of divided partitions 40 is the number of iteration.
- **Round:** the server broadcasts the global model parameters to clients. Then the clients train the model with their data locally, and send updates back to the server. These updates are aggregated at the server and then used to update the global model. This whole process is called one round.

Below is the relationship among epoch, batch size and iteration:

$$one\ epoch = batch\ size \times number\ of\ iterations$$

If the dataset contains 2000 training samples, the batch size is set to 2000. Then it takes one iteration to complete an epoch.

2.4   Variations of Federated Learning

If client A has 60 training samples, during the training phase the batch size and epoch are set to 20 and 5, respectively. Client A has $60 \times 5 = 300$ training samples in total. These training samples are divided into 15 batches, and each batch contains 20 training samples. Fifteen iterations are needed for completing the training phase for client A.

The federated learning process is that at round t, after clients receive the global model $\mathbf{M}^t$ from the central server, they train the model with their full training dataset. For client A, the received global model is optimized 15 times and trained by an unique batch each time. In turn, a 15-time-optimized update to the received model $\mathbf{M}_A^t$ is sent back to the server and aggregated with other clients' results to update the global model as $\mathbf{M}$. Namely, the updated global model $\mathbf{M}$ is a weighted integration of all clients' contributions, including $\mathbf{M}_A^t$.

At the next round $t + 1$, the global model that clients receive is $\mathbf{M}^{t+1} = \mathbf{M}$. $\mathbf{M}^{t+1}$ is more optimized than $\mathbf{M}_A^t$. If client A is still chosen at round $t + 1$, it trains the model $\mathbf{M}^{t+1}$ which is the integration of all clients' contributions at round t. The global model $\mathbf{M}^{t+1}$ at round $t + 1$ integrates all clients' contributions from round 1 to round t as the process moves on.

This paper proposes two variants of federated learning as follows.

One is **epoch-wise federated learning.** At round t, after the clients train the received global model by one epoch, the updates of each client are sent back to the server and then applied for the global model in turn. The updated global model is broadcast again, such as the same clients use another epoch to train the model. In order to distinguish the different rounds, the round t is named as out-round. The round after an epoch trained is named as in-round. In the case of client A, one epoch (60 training samples) is used to train the model for an in-round. During an out-round, five in-rounds are performed (because the number of epoch is set to 5). Since the batch size is 20, each epoch contains three batches. So in the meanwhile, the mini-batch gradient descent optimization algorithm is performed three times. In the next in-round, client A continually trains the model in the same way but with another epoch (same dataset but training samples in a different order).

Another is **batch-wise federated learning**. The learning idea is similar to epoch-wise federated learning but tends to be a little noisier. Instead of training model with the whole dataset or with an epoch, client A in batch-wise federated learning trains the model with a batch in an in-round. During an out-round, 15 in-rounds would be performed on client A for batch-wise federated learning.

The study takes original federated learning as **standard-wise federated learning**. In standard-wise federated learning, there is no in-round. One out-round trains the model with the full dataset. While in epoch-wise federated learning, one out-round trains the model with five epochs; and in batch-wise federated learning, it indicates training with fifteen batches. Because in each out-round the transmitted number of data is fixed, the communication costs of the epoch-wise federated learning and the batch-wise federated learning are five times (number of epochs) and fifteen times (number of batches divided by the full dataset) more than the standard-wise federated learning, respectively. We need to find out, at the expense of communication cost, whether more frequently sharing client updates could improve the performance of a neural network.

3   Experiment

3.1   Experiment Description

Before discussing the experiment results, some experiment settings are classified as follows. Items 1–4 are for the neural network; 5–7 for the training and test datasets; 8–11 for the experiment setting.

1. The artificial neural network used for all experiments has a dimension (784, 128, 10) (784 artificial neurons in the input layer, 128 neurons in the hidden layer, and 10 neurons in the output layer). Thus, this network has 101,632 weight parameters, 138 bias parameters and 101,770 parameters in total.
2. Since the weight parameters of neural networks have to be initialized randomly, an initializer named *glorot normal* is in use, every entry in the weight matrix is a number centered on 0 with standard deviation

$$\sigma = \sqrt{\frac{2}{fan\_in + fan\_out}}$$

   where fan_in is the number of input units in the weight matrix, and fan_out is the number of output units in the weight matrix.
3. All biases are initialized to zero.
4. Although the weight parameters of the neural network have to be initialized randomly, the initial neural networks of all four settings (batch-wise, epoch-wise, standard-wise, centralized) in each configuration are same.
5. The client datasets are all set as balanced. That is, for each round, the training-participants have the same number of training samples. The reason is, if the datasets are unbalanced, in batch-wise federated learning the

optimization process stops when the client with the least number of training samples finishes its training.

6. After the server updates the client to the weighted average, the experiment does not have an influence on the result of standard-wise federated learning whatever the client datasets are balanced or unbalanced.
7. The test dataset consists of 561 samples. It evaluates the seven experiments.
8. The training sample numbers for all four settings in each configuration remains the same, because the neural network performance relies on it.
9. The four different settings complete their training in different rounds, though with the same number of training samples.
10. Two performance metrics for the neural network are in use: accuracy and loss.
11. The experiment results are shown by these two metrics, accuracy and loss vs the number of communication rounds and training samples, respectively.

3.2   Experiment Setting and Results

There are seven experiments in total, their settings are shown in Table 1, and their results are shown in Table 2.

Table 1. Experiment setting

	# client	# epoch	Batch size	# samples	# round (cen.)	# round (stand.)	# round (epoch)	# round (batch)
Exp. 1	10	5	20	65,000			100	325
Exp. 2	30	5	20	165,000			100	275
Exp. 3	50	5	20	240,000			100	240
Exp. 4	30	2	20	64,800			40	108
Exp. 5	30	10	20	312,000			200	520
Exp. 6	30	5	10	145,500			100	485
Exp. 7	30	5	30	126,000			100	140

3.3   Evaluation

There are four figures for each of the seven experiments. They are (1) the accuracy vs the number of rounds; (2) the loss vs the number of rounds; (3) the accuracy vs the number of training samples; and (4) the loss vs the number of training samples. Because the results of all seven experiments are similar, only experiment 1 result is shown in Fig. 2 for the sake of simplicity.

In Fig. 2(a), the number of standard-wise and centralized rounds is set to 20. The number of rounds for epoch-wise is equal to the number of rounds for standard-wise/centralized times number of epochs. The number of rounds for batch-wise is approximately two or three times more than the number of rounds

Table 2. Tab:experiment result

	Setting	# round	# sample	Accuracy	Loss
Experiment 1	Centralized	20	65,000	0.798	0.676
	Standard	20		0.585	1.777
	Epoch	100		0.631	1.619
	Batch	325		0.600	1.467
Experiment 2	Centralized	20	165,000	0.813	0.522
	Standard	20		0.608	1.775
	Epoch	100		0.643	1.609
	Batch	275		0.620	1.471
Experiment 3	Centralized	20	240,000	0.873	0.416
	Standard	20		0.522	1.879
	Epoch	100		0.622	1.690
	Batch	240		0.515	1.585
Experiment 4	Centralized	20	64,800	0.799	0.601
	Standard	20		0.439	2.070
	Epoch	40		0.465	2.049
	Batch	108		0.446	1.981
Experiment 5	Centralized	20	312,000	0.852	0.496
	Standard	20		0.686	1.459
	Epoch	200		0.711	1.230
	Batch	520		0.619	1.197
Experiment 6	Centralized	20	145,500	0.789	0.656
	Standard	20		0.649	1.759
	Epoch	100		0.702	1.551
	Batch	485		0.677	1.154
Experiment 7	Centralized	20	126,000	0.791	0.694
	Standard	20		0.435	2.001
	Epoch	100		0.458	1.878
	Batch	140		0.453	1.886

for epoch-wise according to the number of training samples per client and the batch size.

In Fig. 2(a) and (b), the standard-wise federated learning and centralized machine learning finish the training the fastest compared with others.

In Fig. 2(c), under the same number of training samples, the centralized machine learning achieves the best accuracy, the three federated settings are almost the same, and batch-wise federated learning has the largest fluctuation.

In Fig. 2(d), Under the same number of training samples, the loss of the centralized machine learning decreases far faster than the three federated set-

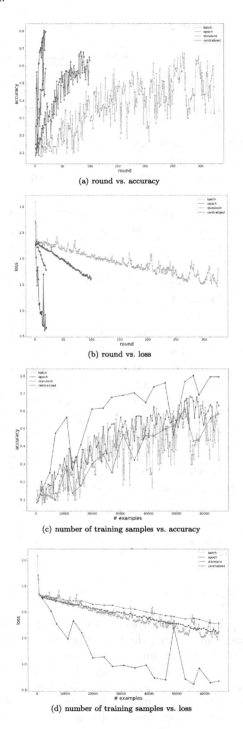

(a) round vs. accuracy

(b) round vs. loss

(c) number of training samples vs. accuracy

(d) number of training samples vs. loss

Fig. 2. Experiment 1 result

tings; among the federated settings, batch-wise federated learning converges the fastest, and standard-wise converges the slowest.

It has been observed that the difference in loss among the three federated settings is more obvious than the difference in accuracy. The reason is that the stochastic gradient descent algorithm used to optimize the neural network decreases the loss function. The response to every iteration optimization is loss change (usually loss decrease, but sometimes loss increase as well because of the stochastic). The accuracy is highly related to the loss, but are not dependent on it. Sometimes the loss decreases, but the accuracy stays or even increases. For instance, assume the desired result is a ten-element vector as $[0, 0, 0, 1, 0, 0, 0, 0, 0, 0]$ representing the label 3 and the predicted result is $[0.5, 0.5, 0.5, 0.8, 0.5, 0.5, 0.5, 0.5, 0.5, 0.5]$, here the loss is equal to 2.29 and the prediction is right. If the predicted result becomes $[0.1, 0.1, 0.1, 0.5, 0.8, 0.1, 0.1, 0.1, 0.1, 0.1]$ after an iterative optimization, now the loss is equal to 0.97 which is significantly decreased, but the prediction is wrong.

4   Conclusion

Edge Federated Learning promises to maintain owner data privacy while achieving effective and timely model optimization. This study analyzes the difference between centralized machine learning and federated learning, as well as the effects of communication frequency between the server and the clients on the learning performance. It proposes two variations of federated learning optimization by analyzing its process. We observed that in the experiments the centralized machine learning often brings a far better training result under the same number of training samples compared with federated learning. Increasing the communication frequency between the server and clients while keeping the number of training samples fixed can improve the learning result.

References

1. Xu, T., Jiang, R., Wen, C., Liu, M., Zhou, J.: A hybrid model for lane change prediction with V2X-based driver assistance. Phys. A Stat. Mech. Appl. **534**, 122033 (2019)
2. Garg, S., Singh, A., Batra, S., Kumar, N., Yang, L.T.: UAV-empowered edge computing environment for cyber-threat detection in smart vehicles. IEEE Netw. **32**(3), 42–51 (2018). https://doi.org/10.1109/MNET.2018.1700286
3. Swarnamugi, M., Chinnaiyan, R.: IoT hybrid computing model for intelligent transportation system (ITS). In: 2018 Second International Conference on Computing Methodologies and Communication (ICCMC), Erode, pp. 802–806 (2018). https://doi.org/10.1109/ICCMC.2018.8487843
4. Zhang, W., et al.: Modeling IoT equipment with graph neural networks. IEEE Access **7**, 32754–32764 (2019)
5. Haller, S., Karnouskos, S., Schroth, C.: The internet of things in an enterprise context. In: Domingue, J., Fensel, D., Traverso, P. (eds.) FIS 2008. LNCS, vol. 5468, pp. 14–28. Springer, Heidelberg (2009). https://doi.org/10.1007/978-3-642-00985-3_2

6. Shrouf, F., Ordieres, J., Miragliotta, G.: Smart factories in Industry 4.0: a review of the concept and of energy management approached in production based on the Internet of Things paradigm. In: 2014 IEEE International Conference on Industrial Engineering and Engineering Management, pp. 697–701. IEEE, December, 2014

7. Chai, X., Hou, B., Zou, P., Zeng, J.: INDICS: an industrial internet platform. In: 2018 IEEE SmartWorld, Ubiquitous Intelligence & Computing, Advanced & Trusted Computing, Scalable Computing & Communications, Cloud & Big Data Computing, Internet of People and Smart City Innovation (SmartWorld/SCALCOM/UIC/ATC/CBDCom/IOP/SCI), pp. 1824–1828. IEEE (2018)

8. Wang, X., Han, Y., Wang, C., Zhao, Q., Chen, X., Chen, M.: In-Edge AI: intelligentizing mobile edge computing, caching and communication by federated learning. IEEE Netw. **33**(5), 156–165 (2019)

9. Konečný, J., McMahan, H.B., Yu, F.X., Richtárik, P., Suresh, A.T., Bacon, D.: Federated learning: strategies for improving communication efficiency. arXiv:1610.05492 (2016)

10. Dean, J., et al.: Large scale distributed deep networks. In: NIPS (2012)

11. McMahan, H.B., Moore, E., Ramage, D., Arcas, B.A.: Federated learning of deep networks using model averaging (2016). arXiv:abs/1602.05629

12. White House Report. Consumer Data Privacy in a Networked World: A Framework for Protecting Privacy and Promoting Innovation in the Global Digital Economy (2012)

13. European Parliament and Council of the European Union: Regulation (EU) 2016/679 of the European Parliament and of the Council of 27 April 2016 on the protection of natural persons with regard to the processing of personal data and on the free movement of such data, and repealing Directive 95/46/EC (General Data Protection Regulation) (2016)

14. Standing Committee of the National People's Congress: Cybersecurity Law of the People's Republic of China (2017)

15. Kairouz, P., et al.: Advances and open problems in federated learning (2019). arXiv:1912.04977 [cs.LG]

Machinery Health Prognostics of Dust Removal Fan Data Through Deep Neural Networks

Tao Yang[1,2]($\boxtimes$), Jigang Wang[3], Liang Chen[3], Zenghao Cui[3], Jianpeng Qi[3], and Rui Wang[3,4]

[1] Central Research Institute of Building and Construction Co, Ltd., Mcc Group, Beijing 100088, China
yangtao0@cribc.com
[2] Beijing Engineering Research Center of Special Substance of Industrial Building, Beijing 100088, China
[3] Computer and Communication Engineering, University of Science and Technology Beijing (USTB), Beijing 100083, People's Republic of China
g20198873@xs.ustb.edu.cn, 18701235329@163.com,
cuizenghao1024@qq.com, jianpengqi@126.com, wangrui@ustb.edu.cn
[4] Shunde Graduate School, University of Science and Technology Beijing, Foshan 528300, China

Abstract. In industrial production, the health of the machine is a very important issue. The health of the dust removal fan is a challenging issue in the field of machine health. In this paper, the deep learning network Variational Auto-Encoder (VAE) and Long Short-Term Memory (LSTM) network are combined to solve the health problem of the dust removal fan. The deep learning network VAE can map the features of the data to hidden variables, and the LSTM network can extract the time dependence between the data. Experiments show that the VAE-LSTM network is suitable for dust removal fans and has a good effect.

Keywords: Deep learning · Dust removal fan · LSTM · Machine health · VAE

1 Introduction

With the development of modern industry, the equipment maintenance problems have been increasingly brought about due to the rapid progress of industrial technology. Manufacturing, high-tech industries and other industries relying on equipment for industrial production have progressively complex equipment systems. Also, due to the complicated operating conditions and poor operating environment of the industrial system itself [1], the performance of equipment is degraded and invalid, then the equipment maintenance has gradually become a new requirement. Traditional maintenance methods often have the problem of insufficient maintenance or excessive, and can not meet the actual maintenance needs based on the actual condition of the equipment. While, with the intelligence of production equipment and the advancement of monitoring technology, the operating parameters of equipment in industrial production are becoming more and more accessible, and these data are gradually being valued by human. With the rise of the data analysis

H. Ning and F. Shi (Eds.): CyberDI 2020/CyberLife 2020, CCIS 1329, pp. 27–37, 2020.
https://doi.org/10.1007/978-981-33-4336-8_3

industry, in order to ensure the safe and reliable operation of equipment systems, modern industries have gradually combined a large amount of data generated during the running process of equipment with reliable data analysis methods [2, 3]. According to complex operating conditions and application scenarios of equipment, the equipment health assessment method is studied based on data.

Using the important parameters collected by sensors and other instruments during the running process of the equipment, building models and extracting features, constructing indicators that can describe the current condition of the equipment to express the change trajectory of the equipment performance, the whole process names health assessment. Combining current monitoring data and historical operating data, this approach can not only evaluate the current status of the system in real time and obtain the trend of system performance changes to pro-vide early warning of failures. At the same time, the health status evaluation can also provide a priori information for the remaining service life of the equipment [4, 5], which is helpful for experts to judge the usability of the equipment. Therefore, the increase in degree of intelligence and complexity of industrial equipment, greatly promotes research on the health of complex equipment.

Among many research methods, deep learning has achieved good performance in many areas due to its excellent deep feature extraction capabilities and the ability to express complex nonlinear relationship where traditional machine learning algorithms perform poorly [6, 7]. Liu et al. [8] used AE to construct a recurrent neural net-work for fault diagnosis of motor bearings. Lu et al. presented a detailed empirical study of stacked denoising autoencoders with three hidden layers for fault diagnosis of rotary machinery components [9]. Zhao et al. proposed the empirical evaluation of the LSTM-based machine health monitoring system in the tool wear test [10]. As an important branch in the field of machine learning, thanks to the rapid development of computers technology in recent years and the active publication of many related algorithm theories, it has made the application scenarios more and more extensive, far-reaching, and effective. However, it's still on the exploratory stage of the research which combines deep learning with equipment health and diagnosis. Unlike traditional machine learning methods that are closely related to industry, deep learning has a shorter development time, more complex theories, a high requirement of the high computing power which make it difficult to combine with actual industrial production.

This paper is based on the actual production data of industrial machines, combined with the deep learning theory, and adopts the VAE-LSTM-based health assessment method. Variational autoencoder refers to an unsupervised neural network model, which can learn the hidden features of the input data. Then it reconstructs the learned new features to obtain the original input data. As a kind of autoencoder, compared with Autoencoder (AE), VAE mainly uses the learned probability distribution for calculation instead of direct numerical calculation. LSTM network can extract the time dependence between data. In this paper, LSTM method combined with VAE modeling is used to study the health status of dust removal fan machine.

This paper is organized as follows: Sect. 2 presents theory of VAE and LSTM network. Section 3 applies the method to a Dust removal fan diagnostic dataset and discuss the results. Section 4 concludes the paper.

2 Theoretical Basis

2.1 Recurrent Neural Network Model

Recurrent Neural Network (RNN) [11] is a neural network which can be used to process series data. Compared with other types of networks, this model has a better effect on processing sequential input data which means that the data before and after own correlation [12]. When the number of neural network layers reaches a certain scale with hidden layers and neuron nodes, theoretically the network can approximate any continuous function with very high accuracy. However, in the face of the above-mentioned sequential data, it's difficult for neural network of the original fully connected structure to perform well without specific means and measures to deal with the correlation. The RNN has a better effect on this type of data. The interrelationship of the sequential data itself determines that if the data is disassembled and analyzed without considering the relationship between each other, a lot of important information will be lost. The RNN uses a special structure to combine the three states before, then and after, so that it can extract features better.

Figure 1(a) briefly shows the form of RNN, while X is the input data in the current state, Y is the output data of the current node, and Y is the hidden layer used to process data, W is weights the same as U and V. In this way, the S of the hidden layer in the RNN would depend on the current input and the S saved by the last node. The parameter W is used to determine the extent of the current impact of the S saved at last time point. Expand the Fig. 1a along the time axis to get Fig. 1b.

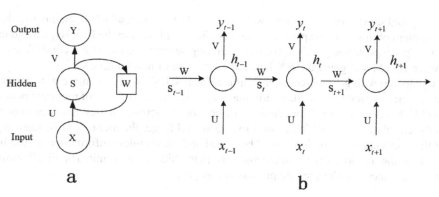

Fig. 1. A form of RNN and process of dealing with data

Figure 1b directly presents the process of recurrent network dealing with sequential data. The hidden layer in the figure is composed of recurrent neuron nodes, where the output data of the node will be fed back to itself and participate in the next calculation. This feedback segment is the core of the recurrent network that can process sequential data. T is the current moment, and the corresponding $t - 1$ and $t + 1$ are the previous moment and the next moment respectively, and h_t is the intermediate conversion node participating in all operations.

At the current time point t, the calculation of the state h_t includes two parts of parameters, one is related to the sequential input data, current input x. The other one is related to the state at the previous moment, that is h_{t-1}. Besides calculating the current input, it also combines the information from the previous sequence. Its specific state calculation formula is:

$$h(t) = f(s_t) = f(Ux_t + Wh_{t-1}) \tag{1}$$

Among them, f is a nonlinear activation function, the parameters U, V, W of the recurrent neuron node won't change with time:

$$y_t = Vh_t \tag{2}$$

The parameters of the RNN neuron node will not change with time, and only the gradient based on the past moment is considered when calculating the gradient during the optimization process. According to the selected cost function, the gradient of the parameters U, V, W of the RNN neuron node is calculated. Recurrent neural networks have advantages in dealing with sequential data indeed, and they have been widely studied. However, some problems were also found during its study, the most important ones were the disappearance of the gradient and the explosion of the gradient. The inability to update the network parameters and the inability of the model itself to converge make RNN unable to process sequential data with long-term dependencies.

2.2 LSTM Model

The long and short-term memory network [13], LSTM, is a special RNN, mainly to solve the problem of gradient disappearance and gradient explosion in the long sequence data training process. It has good performance in long sequence data. The main difference between LSTM and general RNN lies in the structure of neuron nodes.

Compared with general recurrent neural networks, LSTM has one more state parameter C, which is used to store long-term memory as the basic structure of recurrent neural unit [14] described in Fig. 2. In addition, the network structure also designs three to control the circulation unit, which is used to update and forget the memory [15]. Ensuring that the important information would be stored and meaningless information would be discarded, the memory can be stored and flow in the hidden layer unit. The Fig. 2 above can be understood as the specific process below [14]:

The Forgetting-Choosing-Memory Process

For the neuron node at the current time t, the units will process the three inputs data including the input x_t, the states of C_{t-1} and h_{t-1}. The forgotten unit will filter the long-term memory to pick out the important part. Then the input unit control unit will screen the input data and short-term memory. The value of the information itself will directly affect its corresponding weight in the control unit. f_t, i_t, O_t are internal functions that help choosing information. The screening process uses the formula: $i_t \odot \tilde{C}_t$. Among them,

$$\tilde{C}_t = \tanh(W_c[h_{t-1}, x_t] + b_C) \tag{3}$$

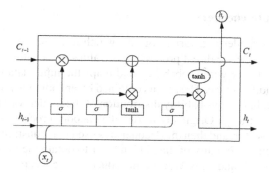

Fig. 2. Basic structure of recurrent neural unit.

Until now, the screening and updating of information is completed. Important information in long-term memory is retained, the short-term memory and current input are also processed. The last step will summarize the information before and determine what the output information is at the next moment, and update the status value according to the following formula:

$$C_t = f_t \odot C_{t-1} + i_t \odot \tilde{C}_t \tag{4}$$

$$h_t = O_t \odot \tanh(C_t) \tag{5}$$

2.3 Autoencoder

The autoencoder adopts the process of encoding and de-coding. After inputting the original data, the encoder learns hidden features, and then the hidden vector is re-constructed into the original input data through the de-coder. Generally, the data obtained after reconstruction will be different from the original input, and the hidden vector dimension in the middle will be lower than the original input data dimension [14]. After the entire encoding and decoding process, the dimension of the recon-structed output vector is controllable, so the important features can be learned, and significant information can be extracted. The entire learning process can be under-stood as the process of minimizing errors of the recon-structed data and the original input data. This unsupervised learning method can also be used for generative models, like generative adversarial networks (Fig. 3).

Fig. 3. Running process of AE.

2.4   Variational Auto-encoder

The variational autoencoder is a variant of AE, which introduces probability statistics based on AE [16]. Unlike the direct processing of values in an autoencoder, VAE combines deep learning theory with probability, and maps the input data to the probability distribution of the hidden space. The results obtained by encoding is no longer the previous encoding vector, but the probability distribution of the hidden variable described by the expectation and variance. Originally in AE, the encoder processed the input data to obtain the encoding vector, and then the decoder was used to reconstruct the input vector, relying on the low dimensionality of the hidden layer to obtain the most significant part of the features. Diederik and Max Welling introduced the concept of hidden variables based on AE, and proposed a variational autoencoder, which uses probability distribution to characterize the range of hidden feature variables. The purpose of training is to learn the mapping function of the encoder and decoder, and find a function optimization goal utilizing variational inference. Based on variational Bayes inference, by searching for the Gaussian distribution satisfied by high-order hidden variables, the high-order features obtained by the mapping usually have stronger robustness.

$P(X)$, the true distribution of the sample, $P(z)$, the prior distribution of the latent variable. $P(X|z)$, the posterior distribution of the sample with respect to the latent variable $P(z|X)$ the posterior distribution of the latent variable with respect to the sample.

To generate a new sample or judge whether a new sample deviates from the normal range, $P(X)$ could be used to sample. But it's difficult to obtain the true distribution of $P(X)$. So, the following formula is needed:

$$P(X) = \int P(X|z; \theta)P(z)dz \tag{6}$$

Sampling to get a hidden vector from the distribution of hidden variables, VAE can use the hidden vector to get the distribution about X. As mentioned above, the hidden space vector will be obtained in the variational autoencoder. Assuming that the posterior distribution of the hidden variable z satisfies the standard normal distribution $P(z)$, then the neural network is used to approximate, $P(X|z, \theta)$. θ is the decoding Parameters. In VAE structure, supposes that the $P(X|z, \theta)$ obey Gaussian distribution, namely

$$P(X|z; \theta) \sim N(X|f(z; \theta), \sigma^2 * I) \tag{7}$$

Through Bayes formula, the goal is converted to $P(z|X)$, which is difficult to solve directly. Currently, it is necessary to use variational inference to approximate its distribution to obtain its approximate distribution $Q(z|X)$. Then Minimize the KL divergence between the two functions.

2.5   Encoding and Decoding Process

The encoding and decoding process of VAE network [17] is shown in the Fig. 4. It's different from the autoencoder in that it does not directly manipulate the input data, but obtains the probability distribution of the hidden variable by calculating the mathematical expectation and variance of the training sample [18]. In the actual training process

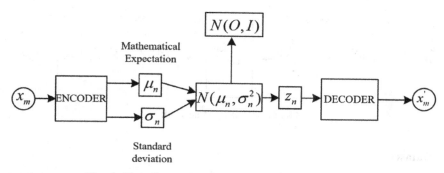

Fig. 4. Encoding and decoding process of VAE network.

of the model, the random sampling process cannot be implemented in back propagation process, which is not conducive to train. In that the proposed reparameterization technique converts the sampling process into the input of the decoder. The sampling process of the original hidden variable z:

$$z = sample(N(\mu(X), \sum(X))) \tag{8}$$

reconstructed to

$$z = \mu(X) + \sum{}^{\frac{1}{2}}(X) * \varepsilon, \varepsilon \sim N(0, 1) \tag{9}$$

For any training sample, the gradient descent method can be used to complete the training of VAE network parameters.

2.6 Proposed Network

This paper applies deep learning networks VAE and LSTM. Through the combination of VAE and LSTM, the health detection of machine is realized. The network structure is presented in Fig. 5. The VAE network includes encoder and decoder parts. The encoder can store the original data in the network structure, and generates a confidence value distribution interval for each invisible parameter, instead of generating a fixed value. The decoder samples the distribution space of each invisible parameter, and finally maps it to the input space. The LSTM network can cyclically operate the information to ensure that the information can be better utilized. The paper takes advantage of the LSTM network to deal with the dependence of time series data and replaces the feed-forward neural network of the encoder and decoder with the LSTM network. Taking machine health data as input, the probability distribution of hidden variables is inferred through the VAE-LSTM model. The VAE-LSTM model decoder then implicitly projects the hidden variables into the input space. The difference between the original input and the mapped output is the machine health value.

3 Experiments Validation

In this paper, a Dust removal fan diagnostic dataset is used for VAE-LSTM network validation, which is from the real industrial production process.

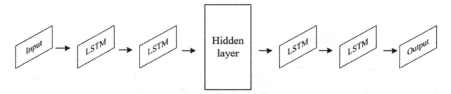

Fig. 5. VAE-LSTM network

3.1 Dataset

The diagnostic data set of the dust removal fan is provided by CENTRAL RESEARCH INSTITUTE OF BUILDING AND CONSTRUCTION CO, LTD, MCC GROUP. The data set contains parts of blast furnace, coking, steelmaking, raw materials, and other parts. Each part contains historical data of dust removal motors and fans. In this paper, the motor-current in the blast furnace is used to verify the validity of the model. There are 53289 pieces of data in total, and the training set, validation set and test set are divided into 80%, 10% and 10% respectively.

Motor-current contains 6-dimensional sequence data. The detailed information of the motor-current data is presented in Table 1, including 6 attributes such as name, type, value, time stamp, quality, and version. The name indicates the name of the current motor, the type indicates the type of collected data, the value indicates the current value of the current motor, the time stamp indicates the time point when the sensor collects the data, the quality indicates the status of the collected data, and the version indicates the version of the collected data system.

Table 1. Motor-current part data

Name	Type	Value	Time stamp	Quality	Version
GL1_1CTC_i_zdj	Int32	131	0:00:00	GOOD	0
GL1_1CTC_i_zdj	Int32	132	0:00:03	GOOD	0
GL1_1CTC_i_zdj	Int32	130	0:00:04	GOOD	0
GL1_1CTC_i_zdj	Int32	133	0:00:05	GOOD	0
GL1_1CTC_i_zdj	Int32	131	0:00:06	GOOD	0
GL1_1CTC_i_zdj	Int32	132	0:00:09	GOOD	0
GL1_1CTC_i_zdj	Int32	133	0:0014	GOOD	0

The motor-current value changes with time and is a time series data. Figure 6 shows the change trend of the motor-current value over time.

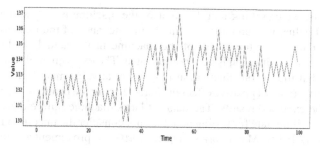

Fig. 6. Motor-current value over time

3.2 Results and Discuss

The VAE+LSTM network includes a 4-layer LSTM network. The first layer LSTM network parameter value is 30 and the remaining three-layer LSTM network parameter values are 60. The input vector dimension is 1 and the output vector dimension is equal to the input. The hidden variable dimension is 60. The LSTM network time step is 2. The experimental environment is developed by keras deep learning framework and python language. TensorFlow is used as the back-end engine. Table 2 shows the parameters of the model.

Table 2. Model parameters.

Parameter	Value
Feature dimension	1
1st-LSTM	30
2st-LSTM	60
3st-LSTM	60
4st-LSTM	60
time-step	2
batch_size	32

According to the previous division of the data set and the setting of network experiment parameters, experiments are carried out on the blast furnace motor-current data in the dust removal fan diagnostic data collection. According to the sliding window method to extract the motor-current sequence data, the time window is 2.

The VAE-LSTM model uses health data as training data. The hidden variables of the VAE-LSTM model learn the probability distribution of health data. Figure 7 shows the test using the motor-current test set as the experimental data to construct the Health Indicator (HI) curve of the motor. The range of HI is 0–1 and the overall value of experimental HI is above 0.6. Since the test set contains health data, the HI curve is not monotonous. The whole curve fluctuates above 0.6. The value of HI is below 0.2.

In some respects, we can think that the wear of the machine is very serious. Through the machine HI value, we can carry out timely maintenance of the machine. Since the data set is the data under the health of the machine in the actual production of the machine, the operation situation is very complicated. The experimental result curves are all fluctuating, but the overall fluctuation range is relatively small, indicating that the VAE-LSTM network has a positive effect in characterizing the health of the machine and has achieved the expected results. The data set lacks machine failure data. This article does not use the failure data for testing and does not consider the uncertain factors in the machine, so the VAE-LSTM network still needs further improvement and improvement.

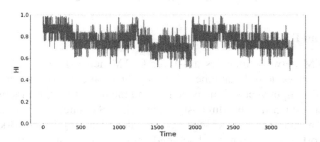

Fig. 7. Motor HI curve

4   Conclusion

This mainly studies the issue of machine health. In the industrial production process, the health of the equipment plays an important role. In response to this problem, we adopted the deep learning network autoencoder VAE and the time recurrent neural network LSTM. The VAE network can learn the probability distribution of hidden variables of the data, and the LSTM network can learn the time dependence of the data.

In order to illustrate the superiority of the VAE-LSTM model, this paper uses the dust removal fan diagnostic data set for testing. In this experiment, the HI curve is used to illustrate the health of the equipment. Experiments show that the VAE-LSTM model is suitable for dust removal fans and performs well.

Acknowledgment. This work was supported in part by Open Fund of Beijing Engineering Research Center of special substance of industrial building, under Grant No. JZA2019KJ04 and the Scientific and Technological Innovation Foundation of Shunde Graduate School, USTB under Grant No. BK19CF010.

References

1. Verma, N.K., Sevakula, R.K., Dixit, S., Salour, A.: Intelligent condition based monitoring using acoustic signals for air compressors. IEEE Trans. Reliab. **65**(1), 291–309 (2016)

2. Jing, L., Zhao, M., Li, P., et al.: A convolutional neural network based feature learning and fault diagnosis method for the condition monitoring of gearbox. Measurement **111**, 1–10 (2017)

3. Su, H., Chong, K.T.: Induction machine condition monitoring using neural network modeling. IEEE Trans. Ind. Electron. **54**(1), 241–249 (2007)

4. Yin, S., Li, X., Gao, H., Kaynak, O.: Data-based techniques focused on modern industry: an overview. IEEE Trans. Ind. Electron. **62**(1), 657–667 (2015)

5. Jardine, A.K., Lin, D., Banjevic, D.: A review on machinery diagnostics and prognostics implementing condition-based maintenance. Mech. Syst. Signal Process. **20**(7), 1483–1510 (2006)

6. Zhao, R., Yan, R., Chen, Z., et al.: Deep learning and its applications to machine health monitoring. Mech. Syst. Signal Process. **115**, 213–237 (2019)

7. Jia, F., Lei, Y., Lin, J., et al.: Deep neural networks: a promising tool for fault characteristic mining and intelligent diagnosis of rotating machinery with massive data. Mech. Syst. Signal Process. **72**, 303–315 (2016)

8. Liu, H., Zhou, J., Zheng, Y., Jiang, W., Zhang, Y.: Fault diagnosis of rolling bearings with recurrent neural network based autoencoders. ISA Trans. **77**, 167–178 (2018)

9. Lu, C., Wang, Z.-Y., Qin, W.-L., Ma, J.: Fault diagnosis of rotary machinery components using a stacked denoising autoencoder-based health state identification. Signal Process. **130**, 377–388 (2017)

10. Zhao, R., Wang, J., Yan, R., Mao, K.: Machine health monitoring with LSTM networks. In: 10th International Conference on Sensing Technology (ICST), pp. 1–6. IEEE (2016)

11. Funahashi, K.-i., Nakamura, Y.: Approximation of dynamical systems by continuous time recurrent neural networks. Neural Netw. **6**(6), 801–806 (1993)

12. Cho, K., Van Merrienboer, B., Gulcehre, C., et al.: Learning phrase representations using RNN encoder-decoder for statistical machine translation. In: Proceedings of the 2014 Conference on Empirical Methods in Natural Language Processing (EMNLP), pp. 1724–1734 (2014)

13. Hochreiter, S., Schmidhuber, J.: Long short-term memory. Neural Comput. **9**(8), 1735–1780 (1997)

14. Chen, Z.: Research on equipment health condition evaluation and remaining life prediction method Based on LSTM network. University of Science and Technology of China, Anhui (2019). (in Chinese)

15. Gers, F.A., Schmidhuber, J., Cummins, F.: Learning to forget: continual prediction with LSTM. In: 1999 Ninth International Conference on Artificial Neural Networks ICANN 99, vol. 2, Conf. Publ. No. 470, Edinburgh, UK, pp. 850–855 (1999)

16. Kingma, D.P., Welling, M.: Auto-encoding variational Bayes. arXiv preprint arXiv:1312. 6114 (2013)

17. Wang, H., Chen, Q.: Power system transient stability assessment method based on stacked variational automatic encoder. Power Autom. Equip. **39**(12), 134–139 (2019). (in Chinese)

Numeric CNNs: CNNs for Reading Numeric Characters on Meters

Hao Xiu, Jie He, Yue Qi$^{(\boxtimes)}$, Xiaotong Zhang, and Long Wang

Department of Computer Science and Technology,
University of Science and Technology Beijing, Beijing 100083, China
`qiyuee@ustb.edu.cn`

Abstract. Nowadays, Internet of Things (IoT) is becoming an irreplaceable role in human life. Moreover, the meter reading is becoming the procedure composed of picture collection and image recognition. Previous works treat meter reading as a problem of image classification. They only focus on the accuracy of classification but ignore numerical accuracy, which is the measurement's essential performance. In this paper, we address that the meter reading is a hybrid regression and classification (HRC) problem. Under this definition, the resulting algorithm considers the targets of both measurement and digits recognition. To solve the HRC problem, we designed a hybrid regression and classification loss function and a multi-branch convolutional neural networks for numbers (N-CNNs). To further verify the effectiveness of the model's classification and regression, we constructed two kinds of datasets: standard dataset and carry dataset. The N-CNNs establishes new state-of-the-art metrics both on regression and classification. Notably, the numerical precision of N-CNNs outperforms the classification-based methods. The numerical accuracy of the model has one order of magnitude higher than other models. Furthermore, we deployed N-CNNs in a realistic meter reading system based on smart meter shells and cloud computing.

Keywords: Meter reading · Internet of Things · Image recognition · Hybrid regression and classification · Convolutional neural network

1 Introduction

In the past 100 years, vast amounts of meters make meter reading become a labor-intensive work and sometimes dangerous work. Besides, the real-time automated meter reading is the fundamental data for energy management. Intuitively speaking, suppliers could replace the analog meters with smart digital meters.

However, the process of digital alteration to meter happens progressively, because of the high replacement cost, the complicated installation process and the problematic data transmission for gas and water meters – the users need to replace billions of analog meters.

H. Ning and F. Shi (Eds.): CyberDI 2020/CyberLife 2020, CCIS 1329, pp. 38–49, 2020.
https://doi.org/10.1007/978-981-33-4336-8_4

Fig. 1. NB-IoT based smart shell for meter reading. The camera captures the meter reading area and NB-IoT module send it to cloud server. The plastic shell is used to cover the meter.

In the last ten years, some researchers have tried to solve the meter reading problem with image recognition However, image data is hard to obtain directly. With the boom of Internet of Things (IoT), short-range-communication technologies [1] are primarily used in small-scale IoT systems. Thus some researchers integrated camera, machine learning recognize the photo on the IoT end node and send the result to the local gateway or edge-computing sever. Such IoT end nodes cannot run typical deep learning networks, and the result cannot be rechecked. Therefore, this kind of solution is challenging to meet the requirement of practical applications. Another intuitive method of meter reading is to recognize the meters' digit based on the photos by smart phone's camera [2,3] and send it to the server via a cellular network. It is not an automatic meter reading (AMR) technology and challenging to be widely utilized.

In recent years, large-scale IoT applications becomes more critical in infrastructure monitoring.

As shown in Fig. 1, we designed a smart shell for meter reading based on camera and Narrow Band Internet of Things (NB-IoT). NB-IoT makes it possible to build a low-cost online automatic meter reading system without meter replacement.

Since NB-IoT connects the Internet directly with acceptable bandwidth and low power consumption, the original photos can be transmitted to the powerful cloud server. Traditionally, the meter reading is considered as a natural sense text recognition problem in the previous studies [4,5] so that researchers only focused on the classification accuracy of the digits. However, a meter is a measurement device, to which numerical precision is the most critical performance. Therefore it is undoubtedly worth introducing numerical precision as a metric to meter reading problem. Considering both measurement and digit recognition targets, we define meter reading as a hybrid regression and classification (HRC) problem in this paper. According to the new problem definition, we proposed a hybrid regression and classification (HRC) loss function and implemented multi-branch convolutional neural networks (Numeric CNNs).

The contribution of this paper is summarized as follows: (1) We defined meter reading as a hybrid regression and classification problem. To the best of our knowledge, this is the first paper considered regression in meter recognition. (2) We proposed a new deep learning model (N-CNNs) to solve this specific problem, which achieved state-of-the-art metrics on numerical precision and classification accuracy in the verification experiments of realistic datasets.

2 Related Work

Automatic Meter Reading (AMR) is a historical problem. In 2007, Graves et al. [6] proposed a loss function named connectionist temporal classification (CTC), which is used to predict on uncertain distance characters. However, nobody applies this method to AMR at that moment when handcrafted feature design was a general method in that time. Traditional methods are almost handcrafted feature engineering, which improved the performance of meter area detection and meter digit segmentation. Some updates are on recognition step by changing the machine learning algorithm, they are [2,7,8], aiming at optimization on recognition algorithm by handcraft. The traditional model always gets good performance on a small dataset. However, the application scale of traditional model was a problem with complex backgrounds, variations of text layout and fonts, and the existence of uneven illumination, low resolution and multilingual content.

In 2015, Deep learning significantly improved the robustness and accuracy of the neural network model. Gómez et al. [9] proposed a segmentation-free system for reading digit text in natural scenes. Their algorithm is different from the progress of the traditional framework, instead of using an end-to-end CNN architecture, directly output the digits of the image, whose architecture is similar to Fully Convolutional Network (FCN). Motivated by CRNN [10], Yang et al. [11] exploited FCN as the CNN components of the network and proposed a public water meter dataset, named SCUT-WMN. To solve the mid-state problem, they compute the *CTC loss* in addition to *Aug loss*, designed for mid-state. Some of the work focus on reducing the computational cost by deep learning. Li et al. [12] proposed a CRNN-based network, whose CNN component is similar to the VGG-16 network, which can decrease the parameters of the model. Similar to this work, Han and Kim [4] also focuses on the size of the model, combining traditional methods and deep learning. To be specific, they exploit the image processing method to pretreat the image and segment the counter area. Then they exploit memory-optimized CNN to recognition single digit. It is noteworthy that the optimized model is only $25KB$ size, which could be run

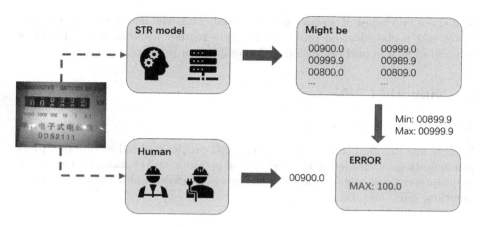

Fig. 2. The carrying state of meter. If we treat the meter image as a nature sense text recognition problem, the result could be: 800.0, 800.9, 809.0, ..., 999.9. The true value should be 899.9 or 900.0. The max error would be 100.0

at Micro-controller Unit (MCU) level devices. However, Laroca et al. [13] follow the traditional steps, dividing the process into two stages, Fast-YOLO for counter detection stage and CR-NET for the counter recognition stage. They also proposed a dataset named UFPR-AMR for future work. The data augmentation technique was exploited to generate a balanced training set. In conclusion, although researchers noticed the regression problem, e.g., mid-state, the previous work focused only on classification accuracy, ignoring the numeric accuracy for the meter reading.

3   Problem Description

The purpose of meter reading is to get the number in meter image. A training set for meter reading problem with labeled instances $T = \{(x_i, y_i, u_i)|x_i \in X, y_i \in \mathcal{Y}, u_i \in U\}$ is given, where X is the input space and $\mathcal{Y}$ is the reading number set, y_i is the i_{th} reading number, $y_i = \{u_i * w_i | u_i \in U, w_i \in W\}$. w_i is the transposition of bit weight vector of i_{th} training data and w_i^j represents the j_{th} bit weight of reading number. $u_i = \{(c_i^1, c_i^2, c_i^3, ..., c_i^n)|c \in C\}$ is a vector composed by m-class classification task. Each task is a classification problem of 0–9, which means $C = \{0, 1, 2, 3, ..., 9\}$. For instance, training data p in Fig 2, $w_p = (10^5, 10^4, ..., 10^{-1})^T$ and $u_p = (0, 0, 8, 9, 9, 0)$.

The equations show that if we treat meter reading as a classification problem and the input is x_t, the output of the classification model should be u_t and the metric for model evaluation should be classification accuracy. If we treat meter reading as a regression problem and the input is x_t, the output of the regression model should be y_t and the metric for model evaluation should be numeric error. However, the users concern both the classification accuracy and numeric error.

And these two types of metrics are not equal. Thus the meter reading problem is not just a classification problem or only a regression problem. It should be considered as a hybrid regression and classification problem.

4   Numeric CNNs

4.1   HRC Loss Function

General loss function could not solve the HRC problem caused by different problem definitions. Considering both regression precision and classification accuracy, we proposed a new loss function named Hybrid Regression and Classification loss function, *HRC loss*, Eq. 1.

$$L_{hrc} = \sum_{i=1}^{n} h_i H(y_i, \hat{y}_i) \tag{1}$$

The h_i means the weight of each classification problem. For meter reading, the high-order digits are more critical because of numeric precision. Moreover, reasoning errors on low-order digits are more sustainable on numeric precision than high-order digits. Thus the high-order digits should gain more weight in the loss. To control the gradient scale, the weight of each hybrid classification problem should be less than 1. The weight settings should obey Eq. 2

$$h_i = \frac{R^i}{\sum_{i=1}^{n} R^i} j \tag{2}$$

The R represents the weight hierarchy of digit, subscript i represents the i power of R. To overcome the dominant gradient problem, the weight hierarchy R should be less than a hyper-parameters λ, which decided by the specific problem, e.g. for meter reading, the $\lambda = 10$ represents the base of the meter number is 10. Thus there are three principles to weight: (1) The size order of weight is the same as the importance order of each hybrid classification problem. (2) The weighted sums of weight are 1. (3) The hyper-parameters λ are not bigger than 10, so that the largest weight can be less than 10^n.

HRC loss function consider the classification accuracy and regression precision together.

4.2   Numeric CNNs

Traditionally, a deep neural network is composed of the CNN layer and the FC layer. The CNN layer is used to extract feature from the image and FC layer is used to classify the feature extract by CNN. In this paper, the model is composed of a new multi-branch network stack with a fully connected (FC) neural network. The architecture of our model is shown in Fig. 3, namely multi-branch conventional neural networks (Numeric CNNs). The number of branches is decided by

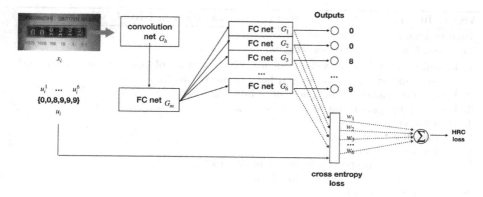

Fig. 3. The architecture of multi-branch CNNs.

the numbers of digit (the numbers of hybrid classification), denoted by n. In this case, $n = 6$. Considering the computation efficiency and the classification accuracy, we utilize Xception [14] as the CNN layer, denoted by G_h. The output of G_h is the n digits' features, which selected by a simple attention network layer, denoted by G_m, which is also an FC neural network. The multi-branch network, denoted by $G_i, i \in \{1, 2, ..6\}$ share same selected features from G_m. The motivation is that the distribution of n digits in images is almost the same. Each FC network G_i has an output encoding by softmax, and each of them corresponds to recognize one digit.

The multi-branch network better than the traditional model because of the following reasons: (1) The multi-branch network is easy to implement and make full use of the *HRC loss* function (2) The multi-branch network can co-judge all the digits of the meter without segmentation and then improve performance.

Among them, W is the parameters of weights in the neural network. For convenience, we simplified the neural network model to $\hat{y}_i = Wx$. When $\hat{y}_i$ and H_i is fixed, the size of the back-propagation gradient *grad* depends on the value of h_i. The larger the h_i is, the larger the back-propagation gradient is, and the corresponding loss value will decay faster.

5   Experiments

5.1   Metrics

In order to evaluate our model, we present five criteria with explanations. Previous researchers have widely proposed a complete accuracy rate. The accuracy rate, MAE, MSE, MAX, are chosen according to the actual application. They are: (a) Accuracy (ACC) is the percentage of the prediction with error <1. (b) Strict ACC (SACC) means that the model identification results are the same as the labeled data or has an error of 0.1. (c) MAX. The value of Maximum absolute error.

Algorithm 1. Pseudo code of one training iteration in HRC-CNNs

---

Input: Training set D nnd the size of D is m.

Output: Update the network weights.

1: Initialize or update all weights in a CNN consisting of convolution net G_h and fully-connected layers G_m and G_i both connected to G_m.

2: Forward propagate all instances of D into G_h.

3: Foward propagate instances of D into G_m.

4: **procedure** HRCLOSS

5:      Initialize total loss $l_t \leftarrow 0$.

6:      **for** $k = 1$ to m **do**

7:          Forward propagate instances of D into G_i.

8:          Calculate the softmax loss l_i of D.

9:          $l_t = l_t + h_i * l_i$

10:     **end for**

11: **end procedure**

12: Backward propagate of l_t

Fig. 4. Carry data set. The meter ends with 0 and 9 is in carrying state. The radio of the figure is on purpose to make the deep learning model more robust. There might be some slope angle on images' views.

5.2   Data Explanation

The size of the raw images from the smart shell is 320 × 240, which is a color image. However, in order to reduce bandwidth consumption during transmission, a gray image was used for transmission. The usage of color images is not as important as other identification tasks like animal and vehicle identification, because the color information for these tasks is a key feature to improve accuracy. For meter reading tasks, images without color could recognize, and the one with color might bring more unusable information to confuse the model. Thus this loss of information is supposed to be acceptable for meter identification.

As it should be, the values of meter readings are also labeled in the data set. The form of the statistics is 00891.2, and the high-order number 0 is reserved, which is suitable for our subsequent processing of the image.

The dataset was divided into a standard data set and a carry data set. Data in a standard data set included the meter reading images of various situations. The sample in the carry dataset is the meter in the carrying state, Fig. 4. The purpose of this kind of design is meant to judge the numeric precision performance of the model. Only the training part of the standard dataset was used to train the model. Both the test part of the standard dataset and the carry dataset is used to test the model's performance. All the images in the carry dataset are used as a test dataset. Wherein, the number of images of the training dataset is 26264, and the validate dataset is 5210. The number of test images in the standard dataset is 5218, and the number of the test datasets is 997.

5.3   Network Training

All networks were trained on an Nvidia TiTAN XP card with ten epochs, and the batch size of data is 32. We implement our network with Keras and Tensorflow. To improve the performance of models, we use two tricks in the training period. (1) A gradient schedule algorithm was applied, dividing the learning rate to 10 after two epochs. (2) Expanding dataset with image augmentation, such as Gaussian blur with the different kernel, image translation, and image rotation, etc. (3) Dumping the weight of neural networks to disk during training, to save the training time. After the data augmentation, almost 100 thousand training data was obtained from the original 26264 images.

5.4   Experimental Setup

To validate our model, We designed nine groups of experiments through the variable-controlling approach. There are three variables in these experiments, including four types of loss functions (UW loss, HRC loss, Avg loss, Cross entropy loss), 3 types of output layers (mLSTM, mFC, FC), whether to use Bidirectional Long Short-Term Memory neural network (Bi-LSTM) module.

The purpose of adopting four types of loss functions lists as follows: (1) UW loss has an excellent performance on the multi-task problem but not validate on meter reading problem. (2) To assess the N-CNNs model, We considered HRC loss. (3) Avg loss is designed to validate the feature of HRC loss, weight tendency. (4) To assess the performance of the one-label neural network, We adopted cross-entropy to train neural networks for classification problems. The outputs of 6 one-label neural network could be encoded to one float number, to validate the co-judgement feature of HRC loss.

The purpose of adopting three types of output layers is to compare the capacities between different neural network's layers to find the best one for the meter reading. The architecture of mLSTM is similar to traditional CRNN [10] in order to compare the previous work. mFC is the output layer of the proposed model to assess the proposed network architecture. Moreover, FC is for a one-label neural network.

Bi-LSTM is a general neural network module for scene text recognition. In previous works, researchers think it could modeling the features efficiently from

Table 1. Experiments for STANDARD DATASET

Network	Name	Loss	MAE	MSE ($*10^5$)	MAX	ACC	SACC
CNN	mFC (bi-LSTM)	UW loss	2412.40	1223.5	52010.1	0.6623	0.6598
	mFC (bi-LSTM)	HRC loss	199.14	69.7	52000.1	0.7711	0.7577
	mLSTM (bi-LSTM)	HRC loss	235.93	97.1	52000.1	0.36415	0.1743
CNN	mLSTM	HRC loss	137.90	2.2	2000.8	0.8815	0.4524
	mLSTM	Avg loss	121.99	54.9	52000	0.9599	0.9570
	mFC(N-CNNs)	**HRC loss**	**8.28**	**0.03**	**600.1**	**0.9630**	**0.9591**
	mFC	Avg loss	24.62	4.8	50000	0.9541	0.9511
	mFC	UW loss	2282.31	1130.6	50990	0.5774	0.5634
CNN	FC	Cross entropy	3104.32	2343.9	78020.1	0.7938	0.7938
-	CRNN[10]	CTC loss	361.14	160.2	46890.1	0.8834	0.8484

Table 2. Experiments for CARRY DATASET

Network	Name	Loss	MAE	MSE ($*10^5$)	MAX	ACC	SACC
CNN	mFC (bi-LSTM)	UW loss	2412.50	1221.1	52010	0.6519	0.6409
	mFC (bi-LSTM)	HRC loss	215.57	75.6	50000	0.7412	0.7081
	mLSTM (bi-LSTM)	HRC loss	146.62	50.4	50000.1	0.3460	0.1725
CNN	mLSTM	HRC loss	142.43	2.3	2000.8	0.8686	0.4523
	mLSTM	Avg loss	224.35	102.9	52000	0.9408	0.9348
	mFC(N-CNNs)	**HRC loss**	**7.06**	**0.03**	**600.1**	**0.9538**	0.9428
	mFC	Avg loss	12.74	0.06	1000	0.9528	**0.9468**
	mFC	UW loss	2276.30	1128.1	50001	0.5987	0.5747
CNN	FC	Cross entropy	3385.3152	2553.6	78020.1	0.7322	0.7322
-	CRNN[10]	CTC loss	392.74	176.5	46890.0	0.8896	0.8535

time and space, to improve the performance on recognition. The Bi-LSTM module is the mid-layers (or decoding layers) in CRNN [10].

5.5 Result

Table 1 and Table 2 show an overview of experiments result. Here is the explanation of the table.

In order to judge the best weight rank R of meter reading, We tested the best integer value of R size from 2 to 10. The best among the values is $R = 2$. Thus the final value h_i is defined in Eq. 3.

$$h_i = \frac{2^i}{\sum_{i=1}^{6} 2^i} \tag{3}$$

First of all, the result of each experiment is the best one under each experiment conditions. We will discuss the features of the HRC loss function firstly and then the network architecture. Table 1 and Table 2 show that on the metrics about classification, e.g. ACC and SACC, model with Avg loss could get a considerably good performance. However, comparing with HRC loss, the result of the model with Avg loss on regression metrics is significant and unstable. To be specific, when we train the model with Avg loss, a phenomenon shows that the changes of Avg loss's training random seed and hyperparameters make the performance on regression metrics volatile. Thus the regression metrics and the phenomenon shows the model with Avg loss cannot control the weight of the different branches.

To compare the performance between Avg loss and HRC loss, Table 2 shows that although HRC loss has a lower SACC than Avg loss, on the other metrics, especially on regression metrics on carrying dataset, HRC loss has a considerably better performance than Avg loss. Therefore, we can conclude that the weight tendency notably decreases the error on regression metrics.

Although Avg loss is not the best result, Table 1 and Table 2 present that Avg loss is better than a one-label model. Thus we could conclude that the co-judgment could improve the performance on classification metrics.

In some of the previous work [10], the Bi-LSTM is a widespread network components. However, from the Table 1 and Table 2, we can see Bi-LSTM does not help for improving the performance of model and the reason might be that Bi-LSTM always is used with CTC loss. In our experiments, the loss number does not decrease after ten epochs, and we think it might because of the local minimum and gradient vanish.

It should be noted that the networks end with LSTM not achieve better performance than the networks end with the FC network. Table 1 and Table 2 display that the mFC is always works well than mLSTM.

Consequently, the proposed model, Numeric CNNs, effectively improved the numerical precision and classification accuracy for the meter reading.

6   Conclusion and Future Work

In this paper, we build a large scale automatic meter reading system based on camera, NB-IoT and cloud computing at first. Special attention was paid to the deep learning model for the meter reading system. The meter reading problem, based on the captured photo, is firstly defined as a hybrid regression and classification problem. We proposed N-CNNs model, which includes HRC loss function and multi-branch CNNs, solve this specific problem. Finally, N-CNNs achieves a state-of-the-art result on metrics designed for meter reading, both on numerical precision and classification accuracy.

However, our model still have some problems. The weight choice depends on handcraft work and there is inevitable gradient dominant problem in the training phase. In conclusion, N-CNNs successfully solved hybrid regression-classification problem and improved the performance of meter reading.

For researchers who want to divide into this problem, we think there still have works to do in the future. Some of them list as follows: (1) Historical data could be introduced to improve the metrics of meter reading. (2) Design a network module to use original weight instead of designing loss. (3) Solve the length problem of CTC loss function. (4) Network perception on the status of scrolling digit, etc.

Acknowledgment. This work is supported by The National Key R&D Program of China, No. 2018YFB0704300, No. 2016YFC0901303, National Natural Science Foundation of China (NSFC) project No. 61671056, No. 61971031, Scientific and Technological Innovation Foundation of Shunde Graduate School, USTB (BK19AF007) and interdisciplinary research project of USTB (FRF-IDRY-19-019).

References

1. Gidlund, M., Han, S., Jennehag, U., Sisinni, E., Saifullah, A.: Industrial internet of things: challenges, opportunities, and directions. IEEE Trans. Ind. Inform. **14**(11), 4724–4734 (2018)
2. Gallo, I., Zamberletti, A., Noce, L.: Robust angle invariant GAS meter reading. In: 2015 International Conference on Digital Image Computing: Techniques and Applications, DICTA 2015 (2015)
3. Elrefaei, L.A., Bajaber, A., Natheir, S., Abusanab, N., Bazi, M.: Automatic electricity meter reading based on image processing. In: 2015 IEEE Jordan Conference on Applied Electrical Engineering and Computing Technologies, AEECT 2015, pp. 4–8 (2015)
4. Han, D., Kim, H.: A number recognition system with memory optimized convolutional neural network for smart metering devices. In: 2018 International Conference on Electronics, Information, and Communication (ICEIC), pp. 1–4. IEEE (2018)
5. Cheng, Z., Bai, F., Xu, Y., Zheng, G., Pu, S., Zhou, S.: Focusing attention: towards accurate text recognition in natural images. In: Proceedings of the IEEE International Conference on Computer Vision 2017 October, pp. 5086–5094 (2017). arXiv:1709.02054v3
6. Graves, A., Liwicki, M., Bunke, H., Schmidhuber, J., Fernández, S.: Unconstrained on-line handwriting recognition with recurrent neural networks. In: Platt, J.C., Koller, D., Singer, Y., Roweis, S.T. (eds.) Advances in Neural Information Processing Systems 20, pp. pp 577–584. Curran Associates Inc. (2008)
7. Vanetti, M., Gallo, I., Nodari, A.: Gas meter reading from real world images using a multi-net system. Pattern Recognit. Lett. **34**(5), 519–526 (2013)
8. Edward, V.C.P.: Support vector machine based automatic electric meter reading system. In: 2013 IEEE International Conference on Computational Intelligence and Computing Research, pp. 1–5. IEEE (2013)
9. Gómez, L., Rusinol, M., Karatzas, D.: Cutting sayre's knot: reading scene text without segmentation. Application to utility meters. In: 2018 13th IAPR International Workshop on Document Analysis Systems (DAS), pp. 97–102. IEEE (2018)
10. Shi, B., Bai, X., Yao, C.: An end-to-end trainable neural network for image-based sequence recognition and its application to scene text recognition. IEEE Trans. Pattern Anal. Mach. Intell. **39**(11), 2298–2304 (2016)
11. Yang, F., Jin, L., Lai, S., Gao, X., Li, Z.: Fully convolutional sequence recognition network for water meter number reading. IEEE Access **7**, 11679–11687 (2019)
12. Li, L., Li, Y., Lian, K., Bian, X., Yang, K., Tian, Y.: PGC-NET: a light weight convolutional sequence network for digital pressure gauge calibration. IEEE Access **7**, 123280–123288 (2019)

13. Laroca, R., Barroso, V., Diniz, M.A., Gonçalves, G.R., Menotti, D.: Convolutional neural networks for automatic meter reading. J. Electron. Imaging **28**(1), 1–14 (2019)
14. Chollet, F.: Xception: deep learning with depthwise separable convolutions. In: Proceedings of the IEEE Conference on Computer Vision and Pattern Recognition, pp 1251–1258 (2017)

DeepTSW: An Urban Traffic Safety Warning Framework Based on Bayesian Deep Learning

Guojiang Shen, Lintao Guan, Jiajia Tan, and Xiangjie Kong$^{(\boxtimes)}$

College of Computer Science and Technology, Zhejiang University of Technology,
Hangzhou 310023, China
xjkong@ieee.org

Abstract. As a part of the smart city, urban traffic safety has always received strong attention. For urban traffic safety, previous work often relies on some additional features and machine learning models, mainly considering whether accidents can be accurately predicted, but these work cannot be well integrated with smart cities. In order to better apply traffic safety warning to smart cities, we propose a traffic safety warning framework based on Bayesian deep learning - DeepTSW. Specifically, we propose a traffic prediction model based on Bayesian deep learning. The regional collision index (RCI) is proposed as the traffic accident risk evaluation parameter, and the gaussian mixture model (GMM) is used to cluster the traffic data to realize the accident risk grade evaluation. The experimental results of actual traffic data show that our traffic accident prediction model is superior to the four baseline models, and DeepTSW can effectively reflect the actual accident risk.

Keywords: Traffic safety · Bayesian deep learning · Traffic prediction · Traffic accident risk evaluation

1 Introduction

With the development of cities, there are more and more urban problems in cities. As a new paradigm, smart cities are promising solutions to urban problems [1]. At present, researchers have made a lot of efforts in smart cities. Smart cities have many applications in urban traffic e.g., Ali City Brain [2]. These applications improve the capacity of urban traffic, improve people's travel efficiency and strengthen traffic safety. The realization of these applications is closely related to traffic prediction and traffic accident prediction. With the continuous development of traffic monitoring equipments and data transmission functions, multi-dimensional real-time traffic data can be collected quickly on a large scale [3]. It is not difficult to find that the data-driven methods are suitable to solve urban traffic problems [4].

Traffic prediction is a key part of smart cities. In traffic prediction, there are many achievements have been made over the years. In traditional, most researchers focuses on analyzing temporal features and building models to predict short-term traffic conditions, which can be roughly divided into two types: parametric e.g., time series [5],

H. Ning and F. Shi (Eds.): CyberDI 2020/CyberLife 2020, CCIS 1329, pp. 50–63, 2020.
https://doi.org/10.1007/978-981-33-4336-8_5

autoregressive integrated moving average (ARIMA) [6] and nonparametric approaches e.g., Support Vector Machine (SVM) [7], k-nearest neighbor (KNN) [8]. However, most of these models cannot analyze complex temporal data, so the accuracy of prediction is a problem. In recent years, rapid data transmission technology and data processing technology have made the development of deep learning a reality. Hinton got a great success in deep learning [9], and many researchers have begun to use deep learning methods. Mobile edge computing allows researchers not to worry about the large demand for computing resources in deep learning [10]. Researchers focus on using deep learning methods to solve traffic problems.

Urban traffic safety evaluation improves traffic capacity and road management [11]. Existing work is dedicated to building models with more dimensions of accident influencing factors e.g., traffic upstream and downstream relations [12] to improve the accuracy of accident prediction. However, for city managers, traffic accident prediction cannot help them manage traffic effectively. Traffic accident prediction is almost impossible to apply to smart city systems.

In this paper, to improve the level of urban safety, we combine traffic prediction and traffic accident prediction to construct an urban traffic safety early warning framework, instead of focusing on improving the accuracy of traffic accident prediction to apply the Smart City system. The occurrence of urban traffic accidents is accompanied by abnormal changes in the traffic conditions of adjacent road sections. We propose a regional collision index (RCI) based on time to collision (TTC) [13] as the link between traffic accident prediction and traffic prediction. We use RCI to classify different risk levels of traffic accidents. Therefore, we can assess and predict the risk of road accidents.

However, there are at least two challenges to achieve a traffic accident risk prediction framework based on RCI. Firstly, RCI is closely related to regional traffic conditions. Existing traffic prediction methods do not consider the spatial correlation of traffic [14], which leads to the low accuracy of regional traffic prediction and the inability to obtain accurate RCI. Secondly, there are few studies on traffic accident risk evaluation [15]. It is a difficult problem to divide traffic safety level.

To solve the above challenges, we propose a framework of urban traffic accident assessment and prediction based on Bayesian deep learning. The contributions of our work can be summarized as follows:

1. We present RCI as the evaluation standard of traffic accident risk, and classify the accident risk into three risk levels with GMM: high, normal, and low.
2. Bayesian deep learning can capture the uncertainty of neural network models. We use Bayesian deep learning to use model epistemic uncertainty to capture problems caused by abnormal data to accurately predict traffic.
3. We use a real-world traffic accident dataset to conduct experiments to evaluate DeepTSW. Experimental results show that DeepTSW can predict accidents accurately and give corresponding risk warnings.

The rest of the paper is organized as follows: Sect. 2 reviews related work. Section 3 described the DeepTSW in detail. Section 4 conducts experiments to evaluate DeepTSW. Section 5 draws conclusions and proposes possible future research directions.

2 Related Work

With the development of deep learning, there are many pieces of research on traffic prediction and traffic accident prediction based on deep learning. Researchers try to overcome the limitations of traditional traffic prediction and traffic accident prediction through deep learning.

2.1 Traffic Prediction

Lv and others use an autoencoder as building blocks to represent traffic flow features and stacked autoencoders to predict traffic flow for the first time [16]. Toncharoen researches the traffic status connection between the upstream and downstream of the expressway, using the data of 40 expressway detection stations combined with Convolutional Neural Networks (CNN) to predict the traffic state [17]. Zhu uses Graph Convolutional Network (GCN) to capture the spatial correlation of traffic and uses the temporal attention mechanism to capture the importance of different time slots, presents an A3T-GCN model for traffic forecasting [18]. Sun and others use stacked gated recurrent units (SGRU) to form a tree structure to adopt the road network for multi-junction traffic forecasting [19]. Zhao captures the spatial and temporal dependence of traffic by GCN and Gate Recurrent Unit (GRU), proposes a T-GCN model for traffic forecasting [20]. Liu and others rely on the Spatio-temporal correlation of urban traffic, use hierarchical attention mechanisms based on BiLSTM combined with temporal clustering to predict traffic speed [21]. Zheng uses meta-GRU as a part of encoder and decoder in ST-MetaNet to explore the temporal correlation of traffic at different times for traffic forecasting [22]. Recurrent neural network (RNN) has good effects on traffic prediction in time series, but it is difficult to solve exceedingly long-term dependencies, because of the RNN error increase as the sequence length increases [23].

2.2 Traffic Accident Prediction

Lu et al. makes a state matrix of real-time weather, lighting, upstream and downstream traffic conditions and uses the state matrix to train the traffic accident prediction model by CNN [24]. Zhao et al. extracts the data features in VANET and uploads the variables to the CNN model trained in the edge computing server to predict traffic accidents [25]. Yuan et al. proposes the Hetero-ConvLSTM framework to solve the spatial heterogeneity of data for heterogeneous data such as weather, traffic, and environment [26]. Ren et al. uses Granger causality analysis to rank heterogeneous traffic accident influencing factors, and presents a traffic accident risk prediction model based on LSTM using ranked factors [27]. Zhou puts attention on heterogeneous data, proposes an attention-based ResNet framework to model the spatio-temporal correlation of data [28].

In summary, deep learning has achieved good results in the field of traffic prediction, but there are few results in practical applications in the field of traffic safety. In this paper, we applies Bayesian deep learning to traffic prediction. We use Bayesian neural network multiple sampling to reduce the influence of abnormal data on the model [29], and combine traffic prediction and traffic risk prediction to propose DeepTSW to provide early warning for traffic safety.

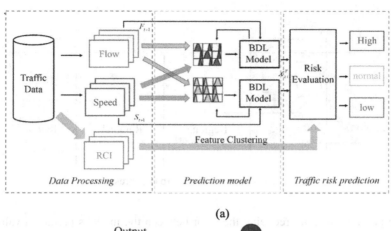

(a)

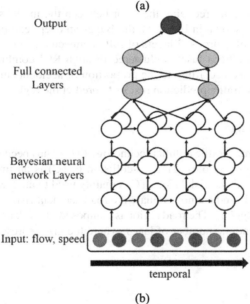

(b)

Fig. 1. The structure of DeepTSW.

3   DeepTSW

As described in Fig. 1(a), DeepTSW takes real-time traffic data as input into Bayesian deep learning model and predicts the region traffic data of the next time slot. Specifically, the data processing module is to calculate the RCI of each region. The traffic data at each time slot is converted into a spatial matrix. Then, the data processing module combines the matrix with different traffic features as input, capture the influence of different features on traffic changes. In the prediction model part, we input the real-time parameters and the set prior probability weights into the Bayesian deep learning model. Through continuous sampling, the model can adjust the weight of parameters

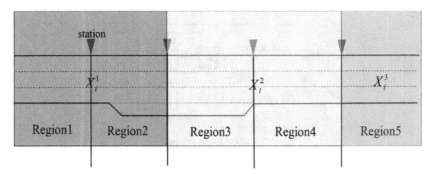

Fig. 2. The region matrix of urban expressways.

through gradient descent, reducing the error between the model's predicted value and the actual value. As shown in Fig. 1(b), the Bayesian deep learning model used in this article has 4 layers of neurons, 2 layers of fully connected layers, and 1 layer of output layer. Finally, the traffic dataset is clustered through RCI combined with GMM, and each cluster is divided according to the proportion of accidents in the actual clustering results and combine traffic prediction results to predict the regional traffic accident risk.

3.1 Data Processing

Problem Statement. Traffic conflict technology (TCT) has been used in different traffic accident prediction studies. Time-to-collision (TTC) is an important indicator for detecting vehicle collision risk [13]. TTC is mainly used to analyze the collision risk of an individual vehicle and cannot evaluate the road accident risk.

Definition 1: (**Region**) The road region is composed of $s \times k$ grid map by the number of road segments and the number of lanes, where the grid represents each lane of each road segment.

Fig. 3. The testing road segment in I110-N.

We regard the vehicles in the road segment as a whole and combine the spatio-temporal correlation of traffic to improve the TTC and propose regional collision index (RCI) to calculate the vehicle collision time of the road segments. For the region r_j, the calculation of its RCI_i will jointly consider average speed v_i in the region and the flow f_i in road segments, i.e.,

$$RCI_i = \frac{\sum_j^d s_j \times k_j \cdot (f_i + \Delta f_{i-1})^{-1} - L}{|\Delta \overline{v_i}|}, \ \Delta \overline{v_i} \neq 0 \tag{1}$$

where s_j is in the number of road segments the region r_j, k_j is the number of lanes in the road segments s_j, f_i is the total flow in i_{th} time in the region r_j, Δf_{i-1} is the number of vehicles that entered the region r_j at the $i - 1_{th}$ time and are still in the region r_j at i_{th} time, and $\Delta \overline{v_i}$ the average speed change in i_{th} time in the region r_j, L is a constant, representing the length of the vehicle.

For traffic prediction, we divide the time series into five-minute segments. For the i_{th} time slot, we use the traffic data in the region to calculate the RCI_i of each region and treat the scattered sections of the road as connected regions which can be denoted by a spatial matrix X_i^T. Figure 2 shows the spatial region matrix.

3.2 The Prediction Model

DeepTSW uses Bayesian deep learning model for traffic prediction. As shown in Fig. 1, the core idea of Bayesian deep learning: the weight of the neural network is regarded as a random variable that obeys a certain distribution instead of a fixed value, and the forward propagation of the network is to sample and calculate from the weight distribution. Next, we introduce the details of each part of Bayesian deep learning. The specific process of the prediction model is shown in Algorithm 1.

Bayesian Theory. Bayesian deep learning completes traffic prediction by calculating posterior probability. For update the weight gradient, Bayesian deep learning use Bayesian theory which concludes prior probability, data likelihood. According to the Bayesian theory [30], for the training dataset $S = (X^T, Y)$ of N inputs x_i and corresponding outputs y_i, we give each input a prior probability interval $p(z)$ and data likelihood $p(S|Z)$:

$$\begin{cases} p(Z) = \prod_{z \in Z} N \ (z \,|\, 0, I), & (2) \\ p(S \,|\, Z) = \prod p(y_i \,|\, f_z(x_i)), & (3) \\ p(Z \,|\, S) = \dfrac{p(z)p(S \,|\, z)}{\int p(S)dS}, & (4) \end{cases}$$

where $N(z|0, I)$ is the individual Gaussian, $f_z(x_i)$ is the output for neural network with weighted input.

Algorithm1: The training method of DeepTSW

Input region traffic volumes and speed: $X_r^T \sim (F_r^T, S_r^T)$

1. **for** k = 1, 2, ... , K **do**

2. $\gamma \sim N(0, I)$

3. Weight $w = \mu + \log(1 + \exp(\lambda)) \cdot \gamma$

4. standard deviation $\theta = (\mu, \lambda)$

5. $f(w, \theta) = \log q(w \mid \theta) - \log p(w) p(X_r^T \mid w)$

6. Calculate $\Delta\mu = \partial f(w, \theta) \cdot (\partial w)^{-1} + \partial f(w, \theta) \cdot (\partial\mu)^{-1}$

7. Calculate $\Delta\lambda = \partial f(w, \theta)\gamma \cdot (\partial w)^{-1}(1 + \exp(-\lambda)) + \partial f(w, \theta) \cdot (\partial\lambda)^{-1}$

8. update $\mu \leftarrow \mu - \alpha\Delta\mu$

9. update $\lambda \leftarrow \lambda - \alpha\Delta\lambda$

10. if $k \neq 1$ and $f(w, \theta) > threshold$ then

11. **end for**

12. save model

There is almost no way to directly find the posterior probability, and the difficulty of calculation increases exponentially with the increase of parameters. Researchers mainly use three methods: approximating the integral with MCMC, using black-box variational inference, using MC (Monte Carlo) dropout. In this paper, we use variational inference to get the posterior probability.

Variational Inference. According to the paper [30], Variational inference uses expert knowledge to construct a distribution $q(Z)$ similar to the posterior probability and then use KL divergence to measure the distance between the two distributions. KL divergence can be expressed:

$$KL(q(Z) \| p(Z|S)) = \log(p(S)) - \text{ELBO}, \tag{5}$$

$$\text{ELBO} = \int q(Z)\log\frac{p(Z)p(S|Z)}{q(Z)}dZ, \tag{6}$$

where ELBO contains the joint distribution $q(Z), p(S|Z)$, and is separated from the posterior probability. Thus, the posterior problem is transformed into an ELBO optimization problem.

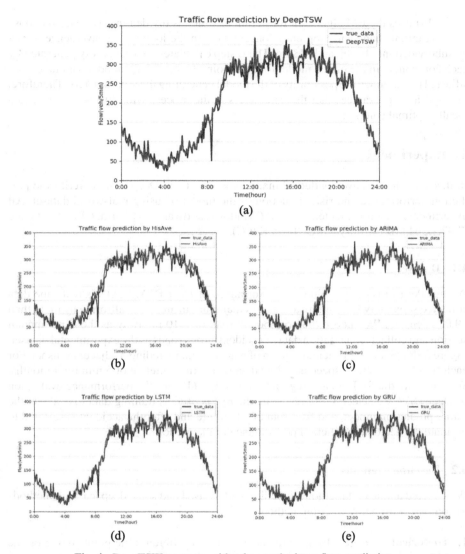

Fig. 4. DeepTSW compare with other methods on flow prediction.

3.3 Traffic Risk Evaluation

We evaluate traffic risk by feature clustering. With the feature clustering of a large amount of data in the dataset, the dataset can be divided into several different clusters. The proportion of traffic accidents in each cluster is different, and traffic risks can be simply divided according to the proportions. Compared with clustering methods e.g., k-means, Gaussian mixture clustering can give the probability that each data point is divided into each cluster, and then we can manually classify some data points that are difficult to classify to improve the classification effect.

GMM uses the EM algorithm for iteration, which is divided into two steps: choose position initial shape and loop until convergence. In the loop until convergence, it can be subdivided into E step and M step. The E step calculates the probability generated by each component in the mixed model for each point. In step M, the model parameters are adjusted to maximize the possibility of the model generating these parameters. Therefore, the algorithm guarantees that the parameters in the process will always converge to a locally optimal solution.

4 Experiment

In this section, we have conducted many experiments on DeepTSW to verify the prediction performance and risk prediction of the model by using real-world dataset. All experiments are implemented on a PC (Windows, software: PyCharm, CPU: Intel Core i7 9700, 64 GB memory, GPU: Tesla K40C).

4.1 Dataset

We use PeMS [31] to evaluate the performance of DeepTSW. PeMS is real-time data collected separately from highways across major urban areas in California by more than 39,000 sensors. We choose the northbound road of I110 highway as the experimental section and collected the station data of accident-prone roads as the experimental dataset. Figure 3 shows an experimental section of nearly 5 km, including 5 adjacent sensors. For each sensors, we obtain speed and flow data with a time interval of 5 min for 4 months, and calculate the RCI of each region based on Eq. (1). For the performance evaluation of DeepTSW, we select 5 h of test data, the rest is used as training data to evaluate the traffic prediction model, and RCI data of 3 h before and after the accident is selected to evaluate the accident prediction performance of the model.

4.2 Baseline Methods

We selected a total of 4 methods including widely used and some deep learning methods to compare with our prediction method,

1. **Historical average:** HisAve predicts the data at different time points based on the historical data of the same factors in the same time period and the same place under the corresponding period.
2. **Autoregressive integrated moving average:** ARIMA is a time series forecasting method that is widely used in transportation and its effect is verified. It realizes forecasting through autoregressive combined with moving average.
3. **Long short-term memory:** LSTM learns the long-term dependence on information and effectively solves the problems of gradient explosion and gradient disappearance by forgetting gates, input gates, and output gates.
4. **Gate Recurrent Unit:** Like LSTM, GRU also achieves long-term reliance on information learning through gating, but compared with LSTM, GRU reduces the number of gates and reduces the computational cost and time cost.

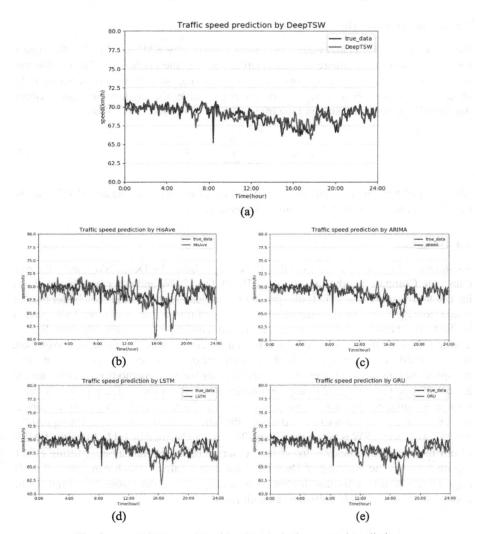

Fig. 5. DeepTSW compare with other methods on speed prediction.

Method Parameter Setting. All models are implemented through the tensor-flow package under python (except for HisAve, HisAve uses the average of 4 1-week-level datas at the same place and time as the predicted value). This package is a python artificial intelligence project with integrated neural network models. The comparative experimental models in this article are all implemented by this package and use the default parameters.

4.3 Evaluation Metric

We evaluate our model and other comparative models by RMSE. RMSE is the square root of the ratio of the square of the deviation between the predicted value and the true value to the number of observations N and is used to measure the deviation between the observed value and the true value. The lower the value, the smaller the error between the model's prediction result and the true value. Its definition is as follows:

$$RMSE = \sqrt{\frac{1}{N} \sum_{i}^{N} (y_i - \hat{y}_i)^2}, \tag{7}$$

where $\hat{y}_i$ is the predicted value at i_{th} time slot of the model, y_i is the actual value at the i_{th} time slot, and N is the total number of predicted values.

4.4 Results

As shown in Fig. 4(a), we can see that the data predicted by DeepTSW can fit the real data well. Compared with Fig. 4(b), (c), (d), (e), DeepTSW and other baseline methods have achieved good results in traffic prediction, indicating that models can better predict traffic flow by capturing the historical periodicity of traffic flow, and DeepTSW predict traffic forecast effective. Traffic speed prediction is different from traffic flow prediction. Traffic speed is affected by traffic at other intersections with close spatial correlation, such as speed, flow, density, etc. In the experiment of this article, DeepTSW considers the speed and traffic of adjacent nodes, while other baseline methods only consider the historical speed or the speed of adjacent nodes. As show in Fig. 5, DeepTSW still has a good effect on speed prediction, and it has a good fit for peaks and valleys. The historical average fitting effect is very poor. Although the other methods have better fitting results, the effect of DeepTSW is better than them. This is also verified in Table 1 that the RMSE of our method is significantly lower than other methods and has a better fitting effect. Figure 6 shows the warning of DeepTSW for traffic safety, which can better classify regional traffic accidents into higher risks, and can accurately assess regional traffic conditions before vehicle collisions as high risks.

Table 1. Comparison among different methods

Method	RMSE	
	Flow	Speed
HisAve	21.44	2.01
ARIMA	18.31	1.22
LSTM	15.56	1.29
GRU	16.29	1.25
DeepTSW	14.67	0.74

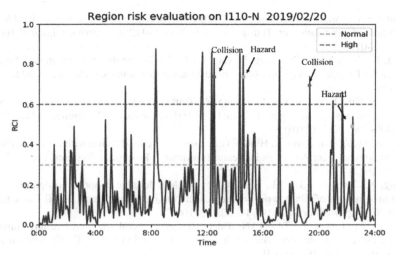

Fig. 6. DeepTSW warn traffic safety by RCI.

5 Conclusion

This paper proposes an urban traffic safety warning framework- DeepTSW suitable for smart cities. DeepTSW adopts a novel RCI metric to measure the traffic accident risk of a region and proposes a Bayesian deep learning based spatio-temporal model for accurately predicting the traffic. Experimental results from real-world traffic data demonstrate that DeepTSW methods can achieve high accuracy of traffic prediction and warn the risk of traffic safety effective.

Acknowledgments. The work was partially supported by the National Natural Science Foundation of China under Grant (62072409, 62073295), and was partially supported by Zhejiang Provincial Natural Science Foundation of China under Grant (LR21F020003).

References

1. Kong, X., Cao, J., Wu, H., et al.: Mobile Crowdsourcing and Pervasive Computing for Smart Cities. Pervasive Mob. Comput. **61**, 101114 (2020)
2. City Brain: Exploring "Digital Twin Cities". https://developer.aliyun.com/article/603873
3. Ma, X., Dai, Z., He, Z., Ma, J., Wang, Y., Wang, Y.: Learning traffic as images: a deep convolutional neural network for large-scale transportation network speed prediction. Sensors **17**(4), 818 (2017)
4. Liu, Z., Huang, M., Ye, Z., Wu, K.: DeepRTP: a deep spatio-temporal residual network for regional traffic prediction. In: 15th International Conference on Mobile Ad-Hoc and Sensor Networks, Hong Kong, pp. 291–296. IEEE (2019)
5. Shekhar, S., Williams, B.M.: Adaptive seasonal time series models for forecasting short-term traffic flow. Transp. Res. Rec. **2024**(1), 116–125 (2007)

6. Kumar, S.V., Vanajakshi, L.: Short-term traffic flow prediction using seasonal ARIMA model with limited input data. Eur. Transp. Res. Rev. **7**(3), 1–9 (2015). https://doi.org/10.1007/s12544-015-0170-8

7. Tang, J., Chen, X., Hu, Z., Zong, F., Han, C., Li, L.: Traffic flow prediction based on combination of support vector machine and data denoising schemes. Physica A **534**, 120642 (2019)

8. Wang, J., Gu, Q., Wu, J., Liu, G., Xiong, Z.: Traffic speed prediction and congestion source exploration: a deep learning method. In: IEEE 16th International Conference on Data Mining, pp. 499–508. IEEE (2016)

9. Krizhevsky, A., Sutskever, I., Hinton, G.E.: ImageNet classification with deep convolutional neural networks. In: Advances in Neural Information Processing Systems, pp. 1097–1105. ACM (2012)

10. Kong, X., Tong, S., Gao, H., Shen, G., et al.: Mobile edge cooperation optimization for wearable internet of things: a network representation-based framework. IEEE Trans. Ind. Inf. 1 (2020). https://doi.org/10.1109/TII.2020.3016037

11. Zhu, L., Li, T., Du, S.: TA-STAN: a deep spatial-temporal attention learning framework for regional traffic accident risk prediction. In: International Joint Conference on Neural Networks, pp. 1–8. IEEE (2019)

12. Basso, F., Basso, L.J., Bravo, F., Pezoa, R.: Real-time crash prediction in an urban expressway using disaggregated data. Transp. Res. Part C Emerg. Technol. **86**, 202–219 (2018)

13. Wang, J., Kong, Y., Fu, T.: Expressway crash risk prediction using back propagation neural network: a brief investigation on safety resilience. Accid. Anal. Prev. **124**, 180–192 (2019)

14. Ma, X., Tao, Z., Wang, Y., Yu, H., Wang, Y.: Long short-term memory neural network for traffic speed prediction using remote microwave sensor data. Transp. Res. Part C: Emerg. Technol. **54**, 187–197 (2015)

15. Liu, Y., Huang, X., Duan, J., Zhang, H.: The assessment of traffic accident risk based on grey relational analysis and fuzzy comprehensive evaluation method. Nat. Hazards **88**(3), 1409–1422 (2017). https://doi.org/10.1007/s11069-017-2923-2

16. Lv, Y., Duan, Y., Kang, W., Li, Z., Wang, F.Y.: Traffic flow prediction with big data: a deep learning approach. IEEE Trans. Intell. Transp. Syst. **16**(2), 865–873 (2014)

17. Toncharoen, R., Piantanakulchai, M.: Traffic state prediction using convolutional neural network. In: 15th International Joint Conference on Computer Science and Software Engineering, pp. 1–6. IEEE (2018)

18. Zhu, J., Song, Y., Zhao, L., Li, H.: A3T-GCN: attention temporal graph convolutional network for traffic forecasting. arXiv preprint arXiv:2006.11583 (2020)

19. Sun, P., Boukerche, A., Tao, Y.: SSGRU: a novel hybrid stacked GRU-based traffic volume prediction approach in a road network. Comput. Commun. **160**, 502–511 (2020)

20. Lu, W., Luo, D., Yan, M.: A model of traffic accident prediction based on convolutional neural network. In: 2nd IEEE International Conference on Intelligent Transportation Engineering (ICITE), pp. 198–202. IEEE (2017)

21. Zhao, H., Cheng, H., Mao, T., He, C.: Research on Traffic Accident Prediction Model Based on Convolutional Neural Networks in VANET. In: 2nd International Conference on Artificial Intelligence and Big Data (ICAIBD), pp. 79–84. IEEE (2019)

22. Yuan, Z., Zhou, X., Yang, T.: Hetero-convlstm: A deep learning approach to traffic accident prediction on heterogeneous spatio-temporal data. In: Proceedings of the 24th ACM SIGKDD International Conference on Knowledge Discovery & Data Mining, pp. 984–992. ACM (2018)

23. Ren, H., Song, Y., Wang, J., Hu, Y., Lei, J.: A deep learning approach to the citywide traffic accident risk prediction. In: 21st International Conference on Intelligent Transportation Systems (ITSC), pp. 3346–3351. IEEE (2018)

24. Zhou, Z.: Attention based stack ResNet for citywide traffic accident prediction. In: 20th IEEE International Conference on Mobile Data Management (MDM), pp. 369–370. IEEE (2019)

25. Zhao, L., et al.: T-GCN: a temporal graph convolutional network for traffic prediction. IEEE Trans. Intell. Transp. Syst. **21**, 3848–3858 (2019)
26. Liu, D., Tang, L., Shen, G., Han, X.: Traffic speed prediction: an attention-based method. Sensors **19**(18), 3836 (2019)
27. Pan, Z., Liang, Y., Wang, W., Yu, Y., Zheng, Y., Zhang, J.: Urban traffic prediction from spatio-temporal data using deep meta learning. In: Proceedings of the 25th ACM SIGKDD International Conference on Knowledge Discovery & Data Mining, pp. 1720–1730. ACM (2019)
28. Yang, B., Sun, S., Li, J., Lin, X., Tian, Y.: Traffic flow prediction using LSTM with feature enhancement. Neurocomputing **332**, 320–327 (2019)
29. Wang, H., Yeung, D.-Y.: A survey on Bayesian deep learning. ACM Comput. Surv. **53**, 1–37 (2020)
30. Blundell, C., Cornebise, J., Kavukcuoglu, K., Wierstra, D.: Weight uncertainty in neural networks. arXiv preprint arXiv:1505.05424 (2015)
31. PMSP Caltrans. http://pems.dot.ca.gov. Accessed 7 Aug 2020

A Multimodal Semantic Model of Packaging Sorting Field Based on Deep Learning

Xuehao Shen[1], Falong Xiao[1], Yuezhong Wu[1,2(✉)], Changyun Li[1,2],
and Honggang Dai[3]

[1] School of Traffic Engineering, Hunan University of Technology, Zhuzhou, China
yuezhong.wu@163.com
[2] Intelligent Information Perception and Processing Technology Hunan Province Key
Laboratory, Zhuzhou, China
[3] China Quality Mark Certification Group Shandong CO., LTD., Jinan, China

Abstract. In order to solve the practical problem of modal gap between different packaging and sorting data in multimodal environment, and not applying traditional machine learning methods directly, by introducing a deep learning feature extraction method, a semantic model of feature representation of multimodal data in packaging and sorting field is proposed based on deep learning. This method proposes a multimodal neural network. For each modal, there is an independent multi-layer sub-neural network corresponding to it. First, converting features under different modalities into features of the same modal, and passing a network layer shared by all modes above these sub-neural networks to establish connections between different modes; then adopting a structured sparse feature selection method to obtain the importance weights of different modalities, and selecting the most important features for the current learning task, so as to eliminate redundant information and noise; finally constructing a multimodal joint shared feature semantic model and applying in the field of packaging sorting. Experimental results show that the proposed model has significant effects and is significantly better than other similar algorithms.

Keywords: Multimodal · Feature extraction · Feature selection

1 Introduction

With the continuous progress of deep learning technology and the rapid development of logistics industry and e-commerce, massive data of various types and different structures have accumulated in the real life and scientific research field [1]. As the name suggests, multimodal information is the general name of the single modal information composed of different information channels describing the same concept or the same problem. Packaging sorting is an essential step in the logistics industry, and sorting goods as a flexible task needs to identify various target objects, locate the position and posture of the objects in a complex environment, and then grab various goods. Using deep learning technology to enhance the value of big data in packaging sorting, first build a multimodal

© Springer Nature Singapore Pte Ltd. 2020
H. Ning and F. Shi (Eds.): CyberDI 2020/CyberLife 2020, CCIS 1329, pp. 64–76, 2020.
https://doi.org/10.1007/978-981-33-4336-8_6

semantic joint feature space to facilitate the future development of visual sorting tasks from simple classification and inspection to more refined and richer intelligent task planning wait for high-level scene understanding.

With the rapid development of information technology today, multimodal data has become the main form of data resources recently [2]. Packaging and sorting big data is a mass of multi-source heterogeneity, although it is easy for human beings to perceive the world by integrating information from multiple senses, how to give machines similar cognitive ability is still an unanswered question. Therefore, it is a very necessary task to study how to extract effective multimode fusion features from multiple modes at the same time by using the data information of multiple modes. However, there are also many challenges in this research task: such as the heterogeneity of multimodal data; the high-dimensional unstructured multimodal data; complementary information will cause the existence of redundant information; the existence of noise information and so on. This paper uses the outstanding results of deep learning in feature expression in recent years and extends it to multimodal feature learning, creatively considering the structural differences and internal connections between different modalities, and effectively exerting the multimodal data itself Finally, a multimodal joint shared feature semantic model is constructed.

The following chapters are arranged as follows: Sect. 2 elaborates on relevant studies; Sect. 3 is model design; Sect. 4 is the analysis of experimental results; Sect. 5 is the summary of the full text and the next research.

2 Related Work

In traditional machine learning methods, feature extraction methods are mainly designed by hand. According to the characteristics of some data modes, the corresponding extraction rules are designed first, and then the original unstructured data are aligned and transformed, so as to obtain the unified features for the next machine learning task. For example, in the related research of computer vision, many image features have been proposed so far. For example, color histogram, directional gradient histogram feature, scale invariant feature transformation and so on. The artificial design of extraction rules for feature extraction solves the problem that unstructured data cannot be applied directly, but the problem of too high data dimension still exists. In order to solve the problem caused by excessively high feature dimension, a dimension reduction method based on many feature transformations is proposed. All these methods map the original feature vector in the high-dimensional space to the new low-dimensional feature space and find the low-dimensional structure hidden in the high-dimensional data. The common transformation methods are divided into linear method and nonlinear method. Linear methods such as principal component analysis [3] and Linear discriminant analysis; Nonlinear methods such as isometric mapping method [4] and local linear embedding method. In 2006, the concept of deep learning was proposed by Hinton et al. [5], which solved the problem of manually designing extraction rules when performing feature extraction in the past. At the same time, deep learning used to extract features also solved the previous problem of feature extraction and feature selection separation. Using a learning model with a deep structure can directly learn high-level abstract features with semantic characteristics from the original data. At the same time, feature learning can directly achieve the effect of dimensionality reduction, and directly learn abstract semantic features with lower feature dimensions.

The current application of deep learning on multimodal data is still focused on multimodal feature fusion. Ngiam et al. [6] first proposed the concept of multimodal learning and introduced multimodal learning into the field of speech recognition. When humans perform speech recognition and semantic understanding, they do not only judge by sound information. At the same time, humans will observe the lip movements obtained in the visual information channel to assist in judging the semantic meaning of the speaker, especially when judging some confusing pronunciations. When discriminating between, the change of the lip shape plays a greater role than the information obtained in the sound signal. Then Srivastava et al. [7–9] proposed a similar depth neural network structure, different coding Ngiam proposed automatic machine, Srivastava RBM employed in the construction of deep neural network as a basic network configuration, and finally form a multimodal depth Confidence network. Similarly, multiple modal information is input into the input layer of the network, and the information of different modalities is transformed into layers of non-linearity, and the final multimodal fusion feature expression is extracted at the top layer. Using this fusion feature expression for image retrieval tasks has achieved very obvious results. At present, there is no relevant algorithm proposed in the field of packaging and sorting, but it is a higher-level processing of data based on semantic analysis. This paper will study the premise of effective reasoning decision based on high-level semantic understanding, which is conducive to the realization of real cognitive intelligence.

3 Model Design

3.1 Overall Structure Design

In order to solve the heterogeneous data structure of multimodal data environment problem, at the same time, in order to effectively utilize a lot easier to get no marks data, this paper proposes a semi-supervised learning algorithm based on depth of learning, from the original data can be effectively provide a variety of different modal extracted from a fusion of low dimensional feature expression, build a multimodal combined share characteristics of semantic mode. Figure 1 shows the overall structure of the multimodal neural network proposed in this paper. The whole structural framework is mainly divided into three parts:

(1) Multimodal deep neural network, the part enclosed by the red dashed box in Fig. 1 is used to integrate different sub-networks to extract more abstract high-level feature expressions from different information modalities and to find different data modalities the relationship between;

(2) Based on the structural sparse feature selection part, it is used to screen the isomorphism features extracted from the lower layer neural network;

(3) The loss model part of the top layer can be set with different calculation models according to different tasks for specific pattern recognition tasks. For example, this article acts on the field of packaging and sorting, so it is set as a classifier model.

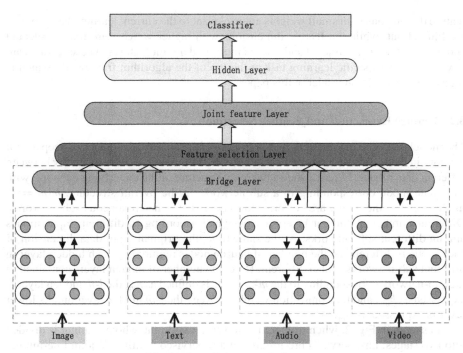

Fig. 1. Overall framework diagram

The multimode neural network is located at the bottom of the whole framework, which is also the core part of the whole algorithm model framework. The multimode neural network is responsible for multiple mapping and transformation of the original data in different modes, and finally extracts the isomorphic features of the same mode. In the lower multimodal neural network, multiple branch networks are included. In Fig. 1, the part in the dashed box of the lowest network allocates a branch of the network for each input information mode, that is, a sub-network becomes the foundation of the entire multimodal neural network. For different modes, the structure of sub-neural networks assigned to them is also different. The number of hidden layers of different sub-networks and the number of neuron nodes contained in each hidden layer are also different.

Different sub-networks in the lower network are used to extract more abstract high-level feature expressions from different information modes, and there may be potential relations between different data modes. In order to find connections between different data modes, a hidden layer is shared at the top of each sub-network of the lower network to connect different data modes, which is called the bridging layer in this paper. BP algorithm [10] is used in the parameter training of the lower network. The function loss defined in the bridge layer is shared by each sub-network and used to adjust each sub-network.

The upper layer of the multimode neural network is based on the feature selection layer with sparse structure. In this part, the optimization weight of each feature dimension is calculated by solving the optimization problem with sparse structure constraints. The feature dimensions with small weights are irrelevant to the current learning task, so they are filtered out, while the feature dimensions with higher weights are finally selected and become the final extracted and filtered multimodal joint features. These features are next used in the specific learning task at the top of the algorithm framework, which is set as the classification model in this paper.

3.2 Feature Extraction and Feature Selection

The model proposed in this paper makes full use of the unique advantages of deep neural network in feature transformation of original data to eliminate the heterogeneity between different data modes. Figure 2 shows the basic structure of the underlying network, with each data mode corresponding to a sub-network. In the overall structure, $m(m = 4)$ modes input in the model are constructed to construct m heterogeneous subnet-works. Different number of hidden layers are designed according to different input modes among different sub-networks. At the same time, the original input data dimension of each mode is different, so the number of neuron nodes required by each hidden layer in different sub-networks is also different. Here, the number of hidden layers contained in the sub-network corresponding to the m-th mode is defined as n_m, the i-th hidden layer is expressed as h_m^i , and the connection weight between the i-th hidden layer and its lower layer is expressed as w_m^i.

As shown in Fig. 2, when training the lower network, the whole training is divided into two stages: unsupervised pre-training and supervised multimode joint fine-tuning. In the pre-training phase, the sub-networks to which each independent mode belongs are trained independently of each other. In order to solve the problem of failure of parameter training for multi-layer neural network using traditional BP algorithm, greedy hierarchical training algorithm is first introduced [11]. In the model structure proposed in this paper, automatic coding machine is used for pre-training layer by layer, as shown in Fig. 3.

As shown in Fig. 3, when training each hidden layer, for the current input x, in the hidden layer, through the weight matrix W_1 and the mapping function $(\cdot)$ do nonlinear transformation, and encode the mapping to obtain the implicit feature expression $h = (W_1^T x)$. A good feature expression should have the characteristic that the original data can be reconstructed by itself. Therefore, in the decoding stage, the weight matrix W_2 and the mapping function $(\cdot)$ are used to reconstruct the original input, and the reconstructed input $x = (W_2^T h)$ is obtained. In order to obtain the coded representation that can reveal the internal structure of the data as much as possible, the optimization objective is the reconstruction error between the original input and the reconstructed input:

$$Loss(x, x') = ||x - x'||_2^2 \tag{1}$$

There is no marked information in the whole training process, so a large amount of unmarked data can be used for unsupervised training.

After the pre-training of independent modes, it is necessary to carry out multimode joint fine-tuning process for the whole network. In this paper, a shared bridging layer is constructed on the top layer of each independent mode's sub-network. The bridge layer connects all the sub-networks to which the modes belong, and the weights between them are T_m. During the fine-tuning process, parameters are adjusted simultaneously with the sub-networks that have completed the pre-training. In order to extract the modal independent features with the same structure from the original data of different modes, the weight connection T_m was made to share the same weight T during the training process.

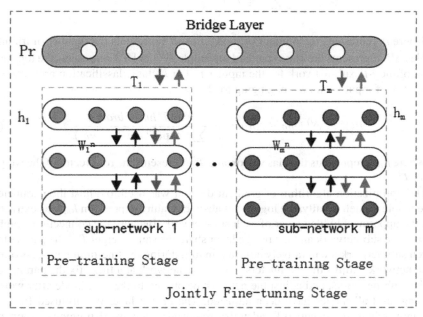

Fig. 2. Schematic diagram of lower network structure

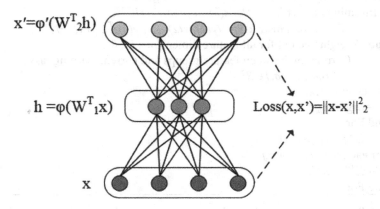

Fig. 3. Sub-networks hidden layer by layer training

It is defined that h_m represents the uppermost neuron of the m-th mode, and Pr represents the label information of the bridge layer. When the whole network is fine-tuned under supervision, the back propagation algorithm is used to optimize the model and the loss function is defined as:

$$L = -\sum_{j}^{m}\sum_{i}^{N} \log(P(Y = y^{(i)} \mid h^{(i)}m, T, b_{root}))$$ (2)

Where m represents the number of modalities, N represents the number of training samples, $y^{(i)}$ represents the class standard of sample $x^{(i)}$, and $h_j^{(i)}$ represents the top-level output of the j-th sub-network for the input $x(i)$. For k class classification problem, the probability of input vector h_m belonging to class i is:

$$P(Y = y^{(i)} \mid hm, T, broot) = \frac{\exp(T^i hm + broot_i)}{\sum \ell \exp(T^\ell hm + broot_l)}$$ (3)

Where b_{root} represents the bias vector, and T^ℓ represents the row vector of the weight matrix T^ℓ.

The optimization algorithm of gradient descent was used to adjust the parameters of the whole model. Finally, the high-level abstract feature expression h_m was extracted from the uppermost hidden layer of each sub-network. Because the connection weights between the sub-network and the bridge layer share the same weight T_m, the parameters of each sub-network are iteratively adjusted in turn during the fine-tuning process of the whole network. Adjust the parameters of one sub-network at a time, fix the parameters of other sub-networks, and adjust the network belonging to the next mode after weight updating until all modes have been adjusted. The bridge layer is only used for joint fine-tuning of the bottom network and will be removed after network training is complete.

Multimodal feature extraction and selection algorithm
Input: training dataset $X = (x(1), x(2), ..., x(n))^T \in R^{n \times p}$,
　　　　Class label matrix $Y = (y(1), y(2), ... , y(n))^T \in \{+1, -1\}^{n \times k}$.
Output: Weight vectors for all feature dimensions $\beta \in R^p$,
　　　　Correlation between feature groups and current learning tasks
　　　　$\sigma = [\sigma_1, \sigma_2, ..., \sigma_g] \in R^g$.
　　For label $j=1:k$
　　$\beta_j := arg\ min_{\beta_j} S(\beta_j)$
　　End For
　　$\beta := \sum_{i=1}^{k} |\beta_i| \cdot p(x=i)$
　　For each feature group i
　　$\sigma_i = (\sum_{j=1}^{Gi} \beta_{Gj}^i)/G_i$
　　End For

Where $P(x = i)$ represents the probability of sample x belonging to category i as the importance weight.

The multimodal depth neural network in the lower layer converts the original different modal features into the isomorphic feature vectors in the same mode, and there are still groups among them. Therefore, this paper chooses the structural sparse method to make feature selection for these refined features. Unless otherwise specified, in this subsection, x represents the refined feature expression obtained in the previous stage. Given training data set $\{(x^{(i)}, y^{(i)} \in R^P \times \{+1, -1\}^k; i = 1, 2, ..., n\}$, n samples with K categories, $x^{(i)} = (x_1^{(i)}, x_2^{(i)}, ..., x_p^{(i)})^T \in R^P$ represents the P-dimensional feature vector extracted from the sample $x(i)$ by the multimode neural network. $y^{(i)} = (y_1^{(i)}, y_2^{(i)}, ..., y_k^{(i)})^T \in \{+1, -1\}^k$ is the corresponding class label. Make $X = (x^{(1)}, x^{(2)}, ..., x^{(n)})^T \in R^{n \times p}$ matrix for training data set, $Y = (y^{(1)}, y^{(2)}, ..., y^{(n)})^T \in \{+1, -1\}^{n \times k}$ indicates the class matrix. Suppose the p-dimensional feature vectors are divided into g feature each groups that do not cover other, and let G_ℓ represent the number of feature dimensions of the first ℓ group. $\beta_j = (\beta_{j1}^T, \beta_{j2}^T, ..., \beta_{j\ell}^T)^T \in R^P$ represents the weight coefficient vector of the j-th category, j represents the sub-coefficient vector of the corresponding group. $X_\ell \in R_\ell^{n \times G}$ is the feature matrix corresponding to the first ℓ group of the training data set.

The feature selection problem for the j-th class can be formalized as the following optimization problem:

$$S(\beta_j) = \min_{\beta_j} L(\beta_j) + R(\beta_j) \tag{4}$$

Where $L(\beta_j)$ represents the loss function, and $R(\beta_j)$ represents the regular term. Depending on the data set and the current learning task, the loss function can be defined in many different ways. This article uses the Logistics loss:

$$L(\beta_j) = \sum_{i=1}^n \log(1 + \exp[-Y_{(i,j)}(\beta_j^T x^{(i)} + c)]) \tag{5}$$

Where c represents the regular term in intercept Eq. 4 which is formally described as:

$$R(\beta_j) = \lambda_1 ||\beta_j||_1 + \lambda_2 \sum_{\ell=1}^g w_\ell ||\beta_{j\ell}||_2 \tag{6}$$

Where λ_1 and λ_2 are the regular term coefficients, and the hyperparameter w_ℓ is the weight of the ℓ feature group, usually set to the square root of the restructured feature dimension size G_ℓ. Make $f(\beta, c)$ said the loss function Eq. 5, define $\phi(\beta)$ for the penalty term in the Eq. 6, the above optimization problem can be defined as the form again:

$$\min_\beta f(\beta, c) + \lambda\phi(\beta) \tag{7}$$

Where the penalty term $\phi(\beta)$ is regarded as a Moreau-Yosida regularization. Liu and Ye [12] proposed an efficient algorithm is used to solve the above optimization problem, and gave the details of the relevant definitions and derivation proof for the optimization method.

3.3 Upper Loss Network

After the high-level abstract expression of each mode is obtained through the bottom network, these isomorphic features are merged in the top network after feature selection, and the final required joint feature expression of multimode fusion is extracted. Figure 4 shows the structural details of the upper network. The upper network consists of three layers: the joint feature expression input layer, the hidden layer for low-dimensional mapping, and the upper classification layer, which is actually a perceptron with a single hidden layer. After feature selection, the isomorphic features obtained by the lower network are first merged into the input X of the upper network, and $h = s(Wx' + b)$ is projected into the low-dimensional feature space after transformation. The classification layer is used to combine unsupervised information and supervised information for parameter optimization of value W.

The classification layer is actually a Logistic classifier. When training the top three layer network, the final loss function is defined as:

$$L = L_{dis} + \beta L_{gen} + \lambda_1 ||W|| \ell_1 + \lambda_2 ||W||_F^2 \tag{8}$$

$$L_{dis} = - \sum_i^N \log(P(Y = y^{(i)} | h^{(i)}, V, b_{top})) \tag{9}$$

$$L_{gen} = - \sum_i^N [x'^{(i)} \log \hat{x}'^{(i)} + (1 - x'^{(i)}) \log(1 - \hat{x}'^{(i)})] \tag{10}$$

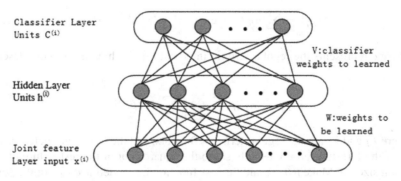

Fig. 4. Schematic diagram of superstructure network

The whole loss function is divided into three parts: L_{dis} with supervision, L_{gen} without supervision, and regular term. The purpose of minimizing discriminative loss is to make the finally extracted multimodal fusion features have strong discriminative ability. Here, Logistic discriminative loss is also used. On the other hand, the extracted fusion features need to have strong generative ability while retaining strong discriminative ability. The generation loss is used to measure the reconstruction loss between the input x and output. A small reconstruction error means that the extracted fusion features retain more original information and the reconstruction loss is defined as:

$$\hat{x}' = s(W^T s(Wx' + b) + b') \tag{11}$$

Where $s(\cdot)$ represents the sigmoid function, and b and b' are bias items.

The weight matrix W is also learned from supervised class standard information and unsupervised reconstruction input. The parameter β is used to balance the discriminative loss L_{dis} and L_{gen}. In order to avoid model over-fitting and at the same time to smooth model parameters, two regular terms are introduced to sparse the weight parameter W. When the gradient descent method is used for the optimization training of the model, the regular term $||W||_{\ell_1}$ is not differentiable at 0, which leads to the failure of the gradient descent method to work normally. Therefore, the approximation of this term is smooth as:

$$||W||_{\ell_1} = \sum_{ij} \sqrt{W_{ij} + \sigma} \tag{12}$$

Where σ is a small positive real number.

4 Experimental Analysis

This article uses public data sets: NUS-WIDE-Object picture text data set; noise speech recognition challenge data set CHIME; video data set COIN. The NUS-WIDE-Object data set contains 30,000 pictures collected from the picture-sharing website Flickr. Each picture is annotated with text tags added when the user uploads the picture. All pictures are divided into 31 categories. Because training a deep neural network requires a relatively large-scale training data set, this article divides the training set and the test set at a ratio of 7:3. When doing unsupervised pre-training of the model, all samples are used for model pre-training. Figure 5 shows a typical form of multimodal information.

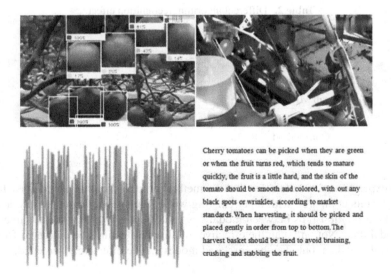

Fig. 5. Multimodal data (image, video, audio and text) of the "agricultural" scene

Table 1. Experimental environment configuration

Project	Experimental environment
System	Ubuntu 16.04 LTS
GPU	NVIDIA Quadro K1200
Hard drive capacity	1 T
Memory	16 GB
Word segmentation system	Jieba Chinese word segmentation system
TensorFlowversion	TensorFlow 2.0
Python version	Python 3.7

The experimental environment configuration is shown in Table 1.

This paper chooses several common multimodal feature extraction methods as experimental baselines for model performance evaluation. (1) SVM, directly splicing data of multiple modalities, and use SVM classifier for classification. (2) PCA + SVM, first splice multiple modal data, use PCA to reduce the dimensionality to 300 dimensions, and then use the SVM classifier to use the low-dimensional features obtained by the dimensionality reduction to classify. (3) Multi-core learning method cab MKLMethod [13]. (4) Unimodal learning method.

As shown in Table 2, this experiment uses accuracy P (Precision), recall rate R (Recall) and $F1$ value (F-measure) as the evaluation criteria for the model recognition effect.

Table 2. Different algorithm recognition effect

Method	Precision%	Recall/%	F1-measure/%
SVM	78.21	75.11	76.55
PCA + SVM	82.54	80.12	81.30
cab MKL	75.45	78.83	77.15
Unimodal	80.54	80.14	80.73
Our method	84.23	81.75	82.94

The experimental results show that the method proposed in this paper has achieved obvious results compared with other existing works. This model can take into account the potential relationships between modalities and effectively utilize the advantages of multimodal data. Not only can the effective multimodal features be extracted from the multimodal raw data, but also the unrelated modes can be effectively screened.

5 Conclusion

The multimodal joint shared feature semantic model proposed in this paper can solve the problem of heterogeneous multimodal data through the feature transformation of deep neural network, and can effectively extract from the original multimodal high-dimensional data while having strong discriminative ability shared feature expression with multimodality of low-dimensional characteristics, creatively considers the structural differences and internal connections between different modalities, and effectively utilizes the advantages of multimodal data. Then, the structured sparse method is used to further select the feature dimensions in the abstract expression, thereby reducing the final feature dimensions. Experiments show that the proposed model has significant effects and is significantly better than other similar algorithms. The next research direction can develop the sorting vision task from simple classification and detection to more refined and richer intelligent task planning and other high-level scene understanding, which may need to rely on the guidance and reasoning of the rich domain knowledge map.

Acknowledgment. This work is supported in part by National Key R&D Program Funded Project of China under grant number 2018YFB1700200, in part by the Hunan Provincial Key Research and Development Project of China under grant numbers 2019GK2133, in part by the Scientific Research Project of Hunan Provincial Department of Education under grant number 19B147, in part by the Project of China Packaging Federation under Funding Support Numbers 17ZBLWT001KT010, in part by the Intelligent Information Perception and Processing Technology Hunan Province Key Laboratory under grant number 2017KF07.

References

1. Baltrusaitis, T., Ahuja, C., Morency, L.P.: Multimodal machine learning: a survey and taxonomy. IEEE Trans. Pattern Anal. Mach. Intell. **41**(2), 423–443 (2019)
2. Chen, P., Li, Q., Zhang, D., Yang, Y., Cai, Z., Lu, Z.: A Survey of Multimodal Machine learning. Chin. J. Eng. **42**, 557–569 (2020)
3. Luo, J., Oubong, G.: A comparison of Sift, PCA-SIFT and surf. Int. J. Image Process. **3**, 143–152 (2009)
4. Tenenbaum, J.B.: A global geometric framework for nonlinear dimensionality reduction. Science **290**, 2319–2323 (2000)
5. Hinton, G., Salakhutdinov, R.: Reducing the dimensionality of data with neural networks. Science **313**, 504–507 (2006)
6. Ngiam, J., Khosla, A., Kim, M.: Multimodal deep learning. In: International Conference on Machine Learning, DBLP 2009, 1230–1440 (2009)
7. Srivastava, N., Salakhutdinov, R.: Multimodal learning with deep boltzmann machines. J. Mach. Learn. Res. **15**, 2949–2980 (2012)
8. Lee, T.S., Mumford, D.: Hierarchical Bayesian inference in the visual cortex. J. Opt. Soc. Am. **20**, 1434–1448 (2003)
9. Serre, T., Wolf, L., Bileschi, S.: Robust object recognition with cortex-like mechanisms. IEEE Trans. Pattern Anal. Mach. Intell. **29**, 411–426 (2007)
10. Liang, F., Shen, C., Wu, F.: An Iterative BP-CNN architecture for channel decoding. IEEE J. Sel. Topics Sig. Process. **12**, 144–159 (2018)

76   X. Shen et al.

11. Bengio, Y., Lamblin, P., Popovici, D.: Greedy layer-wise training of deep networks. In: Advances in Neural Information Processing Systems 19, Proceedings of the Twentieth Annual Conference on Neural Information Processing Systems, Vancouver, British Columbia, Canada, 4–7 December 2006, DBLP 2007, pp. 1159–1367 (2007)
12. Liu, J., Ye, J.: Moreau-Yosida regularization for grouped tree structure learning. In Advances in Neural Information Processing Systems, pp. 1459–1467 (2010)
13. Cortes, C., Mohri, M., Rostamizadeh, A.: Algorithms for learning kernels based on centered alignment. J. Mach. Learn. Res. **13**, 795–828 (2012)

Classification of Autism Based on fMRI Data with Feature-Fused Convolutional Neural Network

Yang You[1], Hongjin Liu[2,3](✉), Shaolin Zhang[2], and Lizhen Shao[1]

[1] Shunde Graduate School, University of Science and Technology Beijing, Beijing 100083, China
[2] Beijing Sunwise Space Technology Ltd., Beijing 100190, China
lhjbuaa@163.com
[3] Beijing Institute of Control Engineering, Beijing 100190, China

Abstract. Autism spectrum disorder (ASD) is a neurological development disorder. Due to the cause of the disease is not clear, the diagnosis of ASD mainly depends on the interactions between individuals and clinical professionals. Functional magnetic resonance imaging (fMRI) has been widely used in the study of brain function in patients with ASD, which provides a new way for the diagnosis of ASD. In this paper, we propose a convolutional neural network (CNN) classification method to classify ASD. The proposed method fuses two kinds of brain functional features, namely brain functional connectivity (FC) and amplitude of low frequency fluctuation (ALFF). Firstly, the two types of feature data which reflect different brain functions are extracted from the fMRI data of ASD patients and normal subjects. Then, CNN is utilized to fuse the two types of data and to predict the classification results. Finally, several experiments are carried out on the ABIDE (Autism Brain Imaging Data Exchange) datasets to test the performance of our proposed method. The fused feature CNN model is compared with the CNN model with only FC or ALFF features; it is also compared with three traditional machine learning methods. The results show that the feature-fused CNN classification model can improve the classification performance to a certain extent; it can be used for computer-aided diagnosis of ASD.

Keywords: Autism spectrum disorder · fMRI · Convolutional neural network · Classification

1 Introduction

Autism spectrum disorder (ASD) is a severe neurological condition that affects social behavior and communication abilities of patients [1]. Although ASD has attracted great attention from many medical scientists, who hope to clarify the pathogenic mechanism of ASD, no effective biological markers have yet been

© Springer Nature Singapore Pte Ltd. 2020
H. Ning and F. Shi (Eds.): CyberDI 2020/CyberLife 2020, CCIS 1329, pp. 77–88, 2020.
https://doi.org/10.1007/978-981-33-4336-8_7

found. The traditional medical diagnosis of ASD is mainly based on the interactions between patients and clinical professionals. This kind of diagnostic method without biological basis may bring many subjective effects [2].

Functional magnetic resonance imaging (fMRI) has been widely used for studying functional activities of the brain. According to recent studies based on fMRI, autistic patients do have differences in brain function from the normal control group, and there are extensive abnormalities in the function of different brain regions. For example, Monk et al. [3] found that ASD subjects had altered intrinsic connectivity within the default mode network, and connectivity between these regions was associated with specific ASD symptoms. Using independent component analysis, Assaf et al. [4] found that ASD patients showed some decreased FCs in default mode sub-networks compared to healthy controls (HC). The magnitude of FC in these regions relates to the severity of social and communication deficits. Keown et al. [5] investigated the local connectivity in ASD and reported that local brain connectivity was atypically increased in autism in the posterior brain. Supekar et al. [6] concluded that children with ASD had shown functional hyper-connectivity across multiple brain regions.

Apart from functional connectivity [7], amplitude of low frequency fluctuation (ALFF) is also a type of key brain-function characteristic data which can be extracted from fMRI data. It also plays an important role in the study of brain function in autism [8]. FC reflects the interrelationship of activities in different brain regions whereas ALFF is used to measure the autonomous fluctuation of blood oxygen signal intensity in the resting state. These two brain characteristics reflect different aspects of brain function. They can both be used for the classification of ASD. At present, there are few studies that integrate these two types of data for the classification of ASD.

Based on fMRI data, lots of machine learning methods have been used to classify ASD and normal controls. For example, Jamal et al. [9] extracted brain connectivity features of 24 children who were handling particular cognitive tasks and used a support vector machine (SVM) to classify autism. Recently, deep learning convolutional neural network (CNN) has achieved remarkable results in the field of image recognition. CNN is a special feed-forward neural network, which has the characteristic of simple structure, high accuracy and wide application range, and it is more and more used in medical image recognition and classification [10]. Li et al. [11] used CNN network to efficiently learn the intrinsic image features from lung image patches and efficiently classify lung image patches with interstitial lung disease. Kisilev et al. [12] proposed a multi-task CNN approach for detection and semantic description of lesions in diagnostic images. The network generates regions of interests surrounding suspicious areas, which can be considered as a medical report for diagnosis. Zhao et al. [13] used the deep CNN framework to learn a spatial overlap pattern in fMRI data in order to discriminate patients with ASD.

In this study, we use both the FC and ALFF feature data to classify ASD. CNN is a deep learning method with good feature extraction and feature fusion capabilities. We proposed a CNN to fuse the two different features. We found the FC and ALFF are complementary for classification of ASD at some extent. The classification performance of the feature-fused CNN is tested on the ABIDE public datasets, and is compared with some traditional machine learning classification methods.

The rest of the paper is organized as follows. In Sect. 2, first, the procedure of data preprocessing and the methods for computing functional connections and ALFF based on resting-state fMRI are introduced. Then we present our proposed feature fused CNN method in Sect. 3. In Sect. 4, we show some experimental results and compare our method with some traditional machine learning methods in the literature. In Sect. 5, we draw the conclusion.

2   fMRI Data Preprocessing

2.1   The Process of Data Preprocessing

The principle of magnetic resonance imaging is to detect changes in magnetic field inhomogeneity caused by changes in blood oxygen. It mainly measures changes in different areas of the brain during the test period, and reflects the measured information as images. The activated blood oxygen level signal is rather weak, and there are many noises. The main noise sources include thermal noise, system noise, rational noise, random neural activity, etc. The system noise comes from the imaging hardware, and the physiological noise comes from the head in the scanner. Differences in mental activity and behavior, including breathing, heartbeat, brain movement caused by the subject's tension or physical reaction, between people also affect the quality of MRI imaging [14]. Due to the presence of these noises, a series of preprocessing must be performed on fMRI before further study. In our experiment, we use the DPARSF2.2 tool of SPM8 software (http://rfmri.org/DPARSF) for fMRI preprocessing. The preprocessing mainly includes:

1. Slice timing: correct the brain slices to the same time point.
2. Realignment: during the image acquisition process, the subject's head may move unconsciously. This behavior will affect the acquisition of brain images. It is necessary to fix the voxels of the brain regions in the same spatial position to reduce the interference caused by the head movement.
3. Normalization: due to the difference in the size of the scanned brain area, the subject's MRI brain imaging size will be different. In order to reduce this deviation, the subject's brain can be projected to the same position in space, that is, properly scaled to the same size.
4. Smoothing: smooth the data to filter out random noise.
5. Detrending: when scanning, the temperature of the MRI machine will gradually increase. The rising temperature will cause a linear drift in the scan results. At the same time, the subjects were gradually stabilized in the scanning environment, which also brought a linear drift. The purpose of detrend is to remove these linear drifts.

6. Filtering: the activity signal of the neuron in the brain is a low-frequency signal, so filtering is to remove high-band noise and to retain the low-band signal.

2.2 Feature Extraction

Functional Connection Matrix. FC is a correlation matrix that can be extracted from fMRI to characterize the interconnection relationship between brain regions [15]. It provides important information for abnormal brain region activity. Brain function connection matrix is widely used in the study of brain function in patients with ASD. Friston et al. [16] first proposed the use of functional connections to measure the correlation between two brain regions. It was found that differences in brain region activity exist.

After preprocessing the data, the brain area can be divided into 116 regions of interest based on the anatomical labeling template (AAL) proposed in [17]. The cerebrum is divided into 90 brain regions. The connection relationship between the regions of interest defined in the brain regions is calculated. By using the connection of the regions of interest as the connections between the brain regions, the connections between the regions of interest are characterized. The flowchart for calculating FC features is shown in Fig. 1. The dimension of the FC feature matrix is 90×90 dimensions. Since the symmetric property of the FC matrix, the lower left triangle elements are used as the FC features.

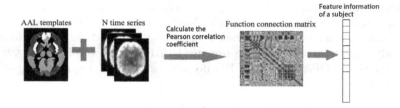

Fig. 1. Schematic diagram of FC feature extraction.

Amplitude of Low Frequency Fluctuation. ALFF measured the power spectrum of blood oxygen activity in the brain area. The ALFF is used to evaluate the physiological state of the brain [18]. For example, the ALFF under the two states of the subject with the eyes open and the eyes closed is obviously different. The results show that ALFF value can reflect different brain states based on the resting state fMRI data. The flow chart of extracting ALFF from fMRI is shown in Fig. 2. The calculation process of ALFF (see Fig. 2) is as follows:

1. Perform 0.01–0.08 Hz bandpass filtering on the time-series signals of each brain region to eliminate the effects of low-frequency drift and high-frequency noise (such as breathing and heart rhythm).

2. The filtered time series signals of the brain regions are converted into frequency domain using the fast Fourier transform. The signals in the frequency domain represent the power spectrum of the brain.
3. The power of a given frequency is proportional to the square of the amplitude of the frequency component in the time domain. The square root of the signal at different frequencies is calculated.
4. Divide the ALFF of each brain region signal by the global average ALFF value as a standardized value. The normalized ALFF value of each brain region signal is close to 1.

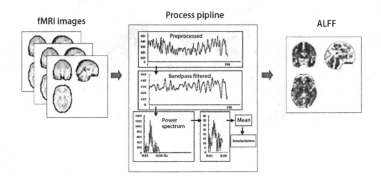

Fig. 2. ALFF feature extraction process.

In the experiment, the ALFF obtained is a 3-D data with the dimension of $61 \times 73 \times 61$.

3   Convolutional Neural Network

The structure of CNN consists of input layer, pooling layer (pool), convolution layer (conv), fully connected layer (FU) and output layer. The role of the pooling layer is to reduce the number of feature dimensions and the amount of network computation. The most common pooling operation is maximum pooling. After passing through the convolutional layer, the data becomes a multi-channel two-dimensional or three-dimensional form, which can be converted into one-dimensional by flattening. The output layer is the fully connected layer to get the final classification results.

3.1   Convolutional Neural Network Models with Different Features

After fMRI feature extraction process, FC and ALFF feature data are obtained. Based on the two different features, we build two different CNN classifiers, one is called FC Net and the other is called ALFF Net. The structure of FC Net has a 6-layer CNN structure, which is composed of four convolutional layers/pooling layers and two fully connected layers. The last fully connected layer has only two neurons, and softmax function is used to achieve the classification of ASD and HC control. The network structure of ALFF net is similar with FC Net. ALFF net is a 7-layer neural network. Because ALFF is three-dimensional feature data, compared to FC Net, the convolution operation is replaced by the operation of three-dimensional convolution (conv3d). The two network structures are shown in Fig. 3 and Fig. 4, and specific parameters are shown in Table 1 and Table 2, respectively.

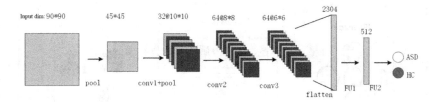

Fig. 3. The structure of FC Net.

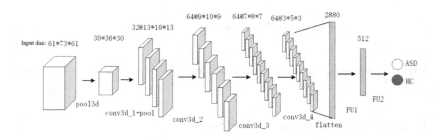

Fig. 4. The structure of ALFF Net.

3.2   Feature-Fused Convolutional Neural Network

In order to extract the effective information from different kinds of features for ASD classification, we propose a CNN-based neural network model with fused FC and ALFF features, which is named as FC&ALFF Net. Specifically, FC&ALFF Net contains two CNN sub-networks (FC Net and ALFF Net) with FC features and ALFF features as inputs, respectively. Each sub-CNN corresponding to a kind of feature is independent of the other. The structures of the two sub-networks are the same as the structure of FC Net and ALFF Net. Each sub-CNN outputs a 512-dimensional high-order feature vectors, and then the feature vectors outputed by the two subnetworks are concatenated as a vector and is feed into the fully connected output layer to predict the final classification result. The structure of the FC&ALFF Net is showed in Fig. 5.

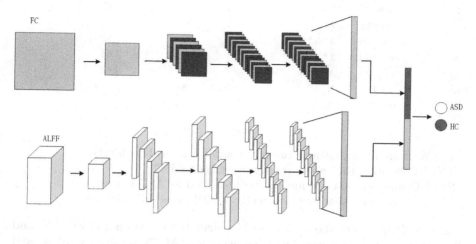

Fig. 5. The Structure of FC&ALFF Net

Table 1. Parameters of FC Net classifier.

No. of layer	Operation	Kernel/pooling size	Stride	Input channels	Output channels
1	pool	2 * 2	2	N/A	N/A
2	conv1	5 * 5	2	1	32
	pool	2 * 2	2	N/A	N/A
3	conv2	3 * 3	1	32	32
4	conv3	3 * 3	1	32	64
5	FU1	N/A	N/A	2304	512
6	FU2	N/A	N/A	512	2

Each classifier is trained 300 epochs. Experiments show that 300 epochs are enough for the classifier to achieve great generalization ability. The activation functions inside the convolutional layers are ReLU function [19], gradient update algorithm uses Adam optimizer [20], and the learning rate is set to be 0.0005.

3.3 Performance Evaluation

There are two categories of predictions outputed by the model: ASD patients and normal subjects. According to the true category of the sample and the label predicted by the model, the sample can be divided into four types: true positive (TP), false positive (FP), true negative (TN), and false negative (FN).

Table 2. Parameters of ALFF Net classifier

No. of layer	Operation	Kernel/pooling size	Stride	Input channels	Output channels
1	pool3d	2 * 2 * 2	2	N/A	N/A
2	conv3d_1	5 * 5	2	1	32
	pool3d	2 * 2	2	N/A	N/A
3	conv3d_2	3 * 5 * 3	1	32	32
4	conv3d_3	3 * 3 * 3	1	32	64
5	conv3d_4	3 * 3 * 3	1	64	64
6	FU1	N/A	N/A	2880	512
7	FU2	N/A	N/A	512	2

- TP: ASD samples that are correctly classified as ASD subjects.
- TN: HC samples that are correctly identified as HC.
- FP: HC samples that are incorrectly identified as ASD subjects.
- FN: ASD samples that are incorrectly identified as HC subjects.

The performance of the model can be calculated based on TP, FP, TN, and FN. The statistical measures, including accuracy (ACC), sensitivity (SEN) and specificity (SPE), are used to analyse the performance of the models. They are given by:

$$ACC = \frac{TP + TN}{TP + TN + FP + FN} \tag{1}$$

$$SEN = \frac{TP}{TP + FN} \tag{2}$$

$$SPE = \frac{TN}{TN + FP} \tag{3}$$

In addition, we uses G-means metric to measure the balance of different categories of the prediction:

$$G - means = \sqrt{SEN \times SPE} \tag{4}$$

4   Results and Discussion

4.1   Performance of Feature-Fused Network Model

In this study, we use the fMRI data from the Georgetown University (GU) and New York University Langone Medical Center (NYU) imaging site in the Autism Brain Imaging Data Exchange (ABIDE) initiative [21] to test the performance of our proposed method. The statistical description of the samples is shown in the Table 3.

Table 3. Description of the datasets.

Imaging site	ASD	HC	Total
GU	51	55	106
NYU	48	30	78

In order to compare the performance of the CNN classification model with different features, we train the three classifiers described in Sect. 3 for each dataset to discriminate ASD. The experimental test strategy uses 10-fold cross-validation, with accuracy, specificity, sensitivity, and G-means as the evaluation metrics. The experimental results are shown in Table 4 and Tabel 5.

Table 4. Classifier performance on GU dataset.

Input features	ACC	SEN	SPE	G-means
FC	55.91%	59.84%	54.50%	0.57
ALFF	64.89%	66.60%	63.19%	0.65
FC& ALFF	**68.54%**	**69.49%**	**67.58%**	**0.68**

Table 5. Classifier performance on NYU dataset.

Input features	ACC	SEN	SPE	G-means
FC	58.75%	68.06%	45.96%	0.56
ALFF	53.13%	63.14%	40.11%	0.50
FC& ALFF	**65.46%**	**67.75%**	**63.14%**	**0.65**

It can be seen from the table that FC and ALFF have certain effects as the discrimination of ASD. Compared with the single feature model, the classification model proposed by this paper has improved the classification performance. Among them, the FC&ALFF Net model has obtained the best experimental results with an accuracy rate of 68.54%. It is proved that the CNN network model can extract useful information from different kinds of information for discriminating ASD. The feature-fused CNN method can effectively improve the model performance. The positive and negative samples of the NYU dataset are imbalanced, causing the SEN value to be a little high.

4.2   Comparison with Traditional Machine Learning Methods

In order to compare the our proposed method with traditional machine learning classification methods, we tested the classification performance of the three machine learning classification methods, including support vector machine (SVM), extreme learning machine (ELM) and K nearest neighbor (KNN) [22]. Each experiment uses ten-fold cross-validation strategy, and the mean of the ten experiments is taken as the final result. The experimental results are shown in Table 6 and Tabel 7.

Table 6. Results of different classification methods on GU dataset.

Method	ACC	SEN	SPE	G-means
Linear SVM	51.36%	50.07%	52.03%	0.51
ELM	55.09%	55.77%	54.87%	0.55
KNN	52.73%	39.67%	51.82%	0.36
Our proposed	**68.54%**	**69.49%**	**67.58%**	**0.68**

Table 7. Results of different classification methods on NYU dataset.

Method	ACC	SEN	SPE	G-means
Linear SVM	70.63%	73.77%	67.25%	0.70
ELM	52.50%	61.76%	36.40%	0.47
KNN	61.88%	77.12%	49.37%	0.62
Our proposed	**65.46%**	**67.75%**	**63.14%**	**0.65**

Compared to the other machine learning method linear SVM, ELM, KNN, the feature-fused CNN method proposed has achieved the highest classification accuracy and G-means value.

5   Conclusion

In this work, we have proposed a fused-feature CNN model which uses both FC and ALFF features to classify ASD and normal controls. Compared to the CNN model only uses FC or ALFF features, the proposed method performs better. The results indicate that the two brain features of FC and ALFF are complementary for classification of ASD at some extent. Further comparison results with the traditional machine learning methods SVM, ELM and KNN also show that the proposed method is better. The proposed CNN model can also be used in other neurological disease classification, such as attention-deficit/hyperactivity disorder and Alzheimer, etc. However, it also needs to be noted that the number of network parameters in the fused-feature CNN model is quite big, and this may bring challenges for training the model.

Acknowledgments. This work was supported by the Scientific and Technological Innovation Foundation of Shunde Graduate School, University of Science and Technology Beijing (No. BK19CE017).

References

1. Diagnostic and Statistical Manual of Mental Disorders : DSM-5. American Psychiatric Association, Arlington (2013)
2. Yahata, N., et al.: A small number of abnormal brain connections predicts adult autism spectrum disorder. Nature Commun. **7**(1), 11254 (2016)
3. Monk, C.S., et al.: Abnormalities of intrinsic functional connectivity in autism spectrum disorders. Neuroimage **47**(2), 764–772 (2009)
4. Assaf, M., et al.: Abnormal functional connectivity of default mode sub-networks in autism spectrum disorder patients. Neuroimage **53**(1), 247–256 (2010)
5. Keown, C.L., Shih, P., Nair, A., Peterson, N., Mulvey, M.E., Müller, R.-A.: Local functional overconnectivity in posterior brain regions is associated with symptom severity in autism spectrum disorders. Cell Rep. **5**(3), 567–72 (2013)
6. Supekar, K., et al.: Brain hyperconnectivity in children with autism and its links to social deficits. Cell Rep. **5**(3), 738–747 (2013)
7. Liao, W., et al.: Endless fluctuations: temporal dynamics of the amplitude of low frequency fluctuations. IEEE Trans. Med. Imaging **38**(11), 2523–2532 (2019)
8. Pan, Z.-M., et al.: Altered intrinsic brain activities in patients with acute eye pain using amplitude of low-frequency fluctuation: a resting-state fMRI study. Neuropsychiatr. Dis. Treat. **14**, 251 (2018)
9. Jamal, W., Das, S., Oprescu, I.-A., Maharatna, K., Apicella, F., Sicca, F.: Classification of autism spectrum disorder using supervised learning of brain connectivity measures extracted from synchrostates. J. Neural Eng. **11**(4), 046019 (2014)
10. Yamashita, R., Nishio, M., Do, R.K.G., Togashi, K.: Convolutional neural networks: an overview and application in radiology. Insights Imaging **9**(4), 611–629 (2018). https://doi.org/10.1007/s13244-018-0639-9
11. Li, Q., Cai, W., Wang, X., Zhou, Y., Feng, D.D., Chen, M.: Medical image classification with convolutional neural network. In: 13th International Conference on Control Automation Robotics & Vision (ICARCV), pp. 844–848. IEEE (2014)
12. Kisilev, P., Sason, E., Barkan, E., Hashoul, S.: Medical image description using multi-task-loss CNN. In: Carneiro, G., et al. (eds.) LABELS/DLMIA -2016. LNCS, vol. 10008, pp. 121–129. Springer, Cham (2016). https://doi.org/10.1007/978-3-319-46976-8_13
13. Zhao, Yu., Ge, F., Zhang, S., Liu, T.: 3D deep convolutional neural network revealed the value of brain network overlap in differentiating autism spectrum disorder from healthy controls. In: Frangi, A.F., Schnabel, J.A., Davatzikos, C., Alberola-López, C., Fichtinger, G. (eds.) MICCAI 2018. LNCS, vol. 11072, pp. 172–180. Springer, Cham (2018). https://doi.org/10.1007/978-3-030-00931-1_20
14. Hallquist, M.N., Hwang, K., Luna, B.: The nuisance of nuisance regression: spectral misspecification in a common approach to resting-state fMRI preprocessing reintroduces noise and obscures functional connectivity. NeuroImage **82**, 208–225 (2013)
15. Di Plinio, S., Ferri, F., Marzetti, L., Romani, G.L., Northoff, G., Pizzella, V.: Functional connections between activated and deactivated brain regions mediate emotional interference during externally directed cognition. Human Brain Mapp. **39**(9), 3597–3610 (2018)

16. Friston, K.J., Frith, C.D., Liddle, P.F., Frackowiak, R.S.J.: Functional connectivity: the principal-component analysis of large (PET) data sets. J. Cereb. Blood Flow Metab. **13**(1), 5–14 (1993)

17. Tzourio-Mazoyer, N., et al.: Automated anatomical labeling of activations in SPM using a macroscopic anatomical parcellation of the MNI MRI single-subject brain. Neuroimage **15**(1), 273–289 (2002)

18. Zhang, B., et al.: Identifying brain regions associated with the neuropathology of chronic low back pain: a resting-state amplitude of low-frequency fluctuation study. Br. J. Anaesth. **123**(2), e303–e311 (2019)

19. Nair, V., Hinton, G.E.: Rectified linear units improve restricted Boltzmann machines. In: Proceedings of the 27th International Conference on Machine Learning (ICML-2010), pp. 807–814 (2010)

20. Kingma, D.P., Ba, J.: Adam: a method for stochastic optimization. In: International Conference on Learning Representations (ICLR) (2015)

21. Di Martino, A., et al.: The autism brain imaging data exchange: towards a large-scale evaluation of the intrinsic brain architecture in autism. Mol. Psychiatry **19**(6), 659–667 (2014)

22. Pedregosa, F., et al.: Scikit-learn: machine learning in Python. J. Mach. Learn. Res. **12**, 2825–2830 (2011)

Ubiquitous and Intelligent Computing

Topic Logistics Based on Node Resource Status

Fu Chen[✉], Yujia Huo, Kun Liu, Wenying Tang, Jianming Zhu, and Weiyu Guo

School of Information, Central University of Finance and Economics, Beijing, China
{chenfu,zjm,weiyu.guo}@cufe.edu.cn, 124222894@qq.com,
LiuKunEmail@163.com, twy178618@163.com

Abstract. The Internet of things (IoT) is an expansion and extension based on the Internet, from network interconnection to the interrelationship of things. Most of the Internet of Things are using the publish/subscribe model, which stipulates the one-to-many situation of nodes in the Internet of Things' uses a publish/subscribe model to achieve communication, using Broker as a relay and topic as a designated transmission path to deliver information to subscribers. But when a large amount of data is being transmitted, there will be node congestion. This will not only reduce the efficiency of data transmission, but also increase and waste the energy consumption of the entire Internet of Things. Therefore, this paper proposes topic logistics based on node resource status, and designs a new network data transmission algorithm. Based on the value of node resource status, it realizes the selection of possible data communication paths. It is verified through experiments that this algorithm can realize node resources. The full utilization of, thereby reducing communication energy consumption and improving transmission efficiency.

Keywords: Internet of things · MQTT · Data transmission

1 Introduction

The Internet of things (IoT) is an expansion and extension based on the Internet, from network interconnection to the interrelationship of things. According to the definition of ITU, the Internet of Things can complete data communication between H2H (Human to Human), T2T (Thing to Thing), and H2T (Human to Thing), using communication technologies such as pervasive computing and intelligent perception to complete the network fusion.

From the perspective of technical architecture, the Internet of Things consists of a perception layer, a network layer, and an application layer. The perception layer includes many different types of sensors and sensor gateways, such as temperature sensors, cameras, humidity sensors, GPS, RFID tags, etc., to complete the identification, acquisition and collection of information similar to a human perception system. The application layer realizes the application connection of the Internet of Things according to the different needs of the application industry. It is based on this that the Internet of Things can be widely used in various fields such as agriculture, cities, and medical care to realize intelligent applications.

© Springer Nature Singapore Pte Ltd. 2020
H. Ning and F. Shi (Eds.): CyberDI 2020/CyberLife 2020, CCIS 1329, pp. 91–102, 2020.
https://doi.org/10.1007/978-981-33-4336-8_8

The core of the Internet of Things is device communication. Several common communication protocols are Message Queuing Telemetry Transport (MQTT), SigFox, HyperText Transfer Protocol (HTTP), XMPP, WebSocket, The Constrained Application Protocol(TCOAP) and so on. Since the Internet of Things is built on the basis of the Internet, protocols such as HTTP, XMPP, and websocket have been used in Internet of Things communications. HTTP protocol is a typical CS communication mode with low development cost; Websocket exists as a supplement to HTTP; XMPP protocol based on XML has higher availability and lower development cost compared with HTTP.COAP protocol is specially designed for low-power communication of IoT devices. It uses UDP instead of TCP to reduce overhead, binary compression to reduce data volume, and asynchronous transmission to increase response rate. MQTT protocol matures earlier than COAP protocol. Reliable communication provides an instant communication protocol based on TCP, which is suitable for any platform, and can realize the connection between all items in the network and the outside. The choice of agreement is usually carried out according to different factors such as the type of business.

Most of the Internet of Things are using the publish/subscribe model to determine the node dependency by specifying the one-to-many situation of nodes in the Internet of Things. This mode is mainly used between servers and devices, and relies on a central broker to complete the operation of the program. MQTT uses a publish/subscribe model to achieve communication, using Broker as a relay and topic as a designated transmission path to deliver information to subscribers.

Data acquisition in the Internet of Things starts from edge sensors, microcomputers, etc. in real time, and uses topic "channels" to transmit data and store them in the cloud to realize data visualization. In this case, when a large amount of data is being transmitted, there will be node congestion. This will not only reduce the efficiency of data transmission, but also increase and waste the energy consumption of the entire Internet of Things. Therefore, this paper proposes topic logistics based on node resource status and designs a new network data transmission algorithm. The main academic contributions of this paper are as follows:

Analyze the problems existing in the data communication of the existing Internet of Things;
Analyze and design and implement the communication path selection algorithm for the new entry node based on the node resource status;
Analyze and design the communication path selection algorithm for existing nodes based on the node resource status.

The main structure of this paper is as follows: The first section introduces the background of the research and related theoretical basic knowledge; the second section introduces the research progress in related fields; the third section analyzes and designs and implements new data communication algorithms; The algorithm proposed in the third section is analyzed and implemented; the fifth section is a summary of the full text.

2 Related Work

The communication protocol is the key core of the Internet of Things communication, and the innovation of the protocol at home and abroad is very extensive. Paper [1] emphasized the importance of the MQTT protocol in the Internet of Things, and made a detailed introduction from its architecture, application fields, existing problems and development prospects; paper [2] proposed and introduced the MQTT-SN 1.2 version in detail, which is based on the market popularity of WSN to realize the application in the wireless communication environment; paper [3] proposed a model of MQTT version 3.1 and described it by process algebra; paper [4] introduces the features, message mode, nature and application of MQTT 5.0 version; paper [5] introduces the MQTT-SN version, paper [6] proposes a new MQTT protocol that changes the way of data transmission MQTT-EA, paper [7] describes PMQTT, which contains encryption primitives and can be Networking provides more secure services.

For the research on the performance of the Internet of Things, paper [8] achieved the reduction of overhead and memory usage by integrating MQTT and QUIC; Paper [9] designed and published the MQTT protocol logic model to reduce information loss and information explosion problems; paper [10] proposes that the message buffer is used as a data transmission medium to improve the traditional publish/subscribe protocol, optimize device connection, and ensure the integrity of data transmission; paper [11] uses the "Value-to-HMAC" method to maximize confidentiality and integrity by allowing only the target node to read the message while ensuring performance to the greatest extent; paper [12] implements data collection and traffic anomaly analysis through five steps to further analyze traffic behavior; paper [13] proposed the concept of Opportunistic Context-Virtual Networks (OCVN). Compared with other opportunistic routing algorithms, both the transmission efficiency and the energy cost are greatly reduced.

In the real application of the Internet of Things, in addition to paper [14] for environmental monitoring, paper [15] for automatic irrigation monitoring, paper [16] for vehicle communication, paper [17] and paper [18] for aircraft In addition to in-flight data transmission, research on the Internet of Opportunities is also constantly being carried out. Paper [19] analyzes the nature of opportunism through modeling and uses aggregate computing to realize simulation services, and verifies its huge potential through the research and application of the real case of urban population; paper [20] combines the Opportunity Internet of Things with animal husbandry, and verifies the effectiveness of farmers' use of data and the availability of operating cloud platforms by monitoring and studying the cattle-grazing system in a large free pastoral area; paper [21] is applied to Internet of Underwater Things (IoUT) opportunistic routing protocol based on power control, which improves transmission efficiency and reduces energy consumption costs; paper [22] aims at the UAV Internet of Things (IoDT) and uses edge computing to propose the concept of "Edge Drone", which integrates IoT and Ad-Hoc to reduce energy consumption.

3 Data Communication Algorithm Design

3.1 Analysis of Existing Problems

In order to realize the communication among many nodes in the huge network system of the Internet of Things, the problem of energy consumption cannot be ignored [8, 13]. In the existing Internet of Things, the process of data communication may have the following problems: First, when the amount of data that needs to be transmitted is huge or malicious nodes conduct malicious attacks by sending messages, node blockage may occur during data transmission. This reduces the data transmission efficiency to a certain extent and increases the energy consumption in the network; second, when most of the data transmission is undertaken by a certain part of the node, there is bound to be another part of unused nodes, which will cause a certain degree of waste of energy.

3.2 New Algorithm Analysis and Design

Aiming at the problems raised and analyzed in Sect. 3.1, this paper based on the node resource status, using the idea of Markov Chain Monte Carlo Chain Random Walk Algorithm (MCMC), and proposed a new data communication algorithm. In the Internet of Things, sensor nodes are connected to each other to form Directed Acyclic Graph (DAG), and are connected to the same type of Broker, and finally to Broker0. Through data acquisition and data transmission, real-time data visualization and cloud platform storage of the entire network can be realized.

Each sensor node has a resource status data. The data value is composed of the node's default initial state value 1 and other sensor nodes that use the node as a data transmission path, that is, the number of other sensor nodes that directly point to the sensor node, and the number of other sensor nodes that indirectly point to the sensor node. The sum of the three is the existing resource state value of the node. When the number of sensor nodes directly or indirectly connected to the node increases, the resource state value of the node also increases. The node resource status value reflects the current resource status of the node. The larger the resource status value, the busier the current node, and the smaller the resource status value, the more idle the current node. A node with a small resource state value can be used as one of the first node selection paths considered, and the probability of being selected is greater. When a sensor node needs to communicate, it will use the Markov chain Monte Carlo random walk algorithm idea to plan the data transmission route based on the resource status of the selectable node in the current state, avoid congestion, and improve the data transmission efficiency.

3.3 Newcomer Communication Path Selection Algorithm

In the Internet of Things, when a new entry node wants to join the network, first, you need to enter the node name and the Broker category that the node will join. Under this category, starting from Broker0 by introducing a "walking aid", based on the resource state value, in the state of judging whether the optional node is alive, the node connection path is the available path for future data communication. The specific code is shown in Algorithm 1.

Algorithm 1 New entry node communication path selection algorithm

Input: sensor node name, Broker category to which the sensor node belongs

Output: The connection path of the sensor node is the available path for future data communication

   1. According to the Broker category the sensor node belongs to, determine the available networks

   2. Determine whether the Broker in this category is alive

     (1) If the type of Broker survives, start from Broker0, look up the connection status of the node where the "walker" is located, and get the available connection nodes

      ①If there are connected nodes, judge the survival status of all connected nodes

       A. If the node is alive, record the resource status value of the node

        a. Through the established formula, calculate the sum of the resource state values of all nodes that can be selected and the probability that each node may be selected. The larger the resource state value, the smaller the probability of the node being selected

        b. Determine the node selection through random walk, record and output the selection result

       B. If the node is not alive, then give up the node

      ② If there is no connection node, the node can be directly connected to the new incoming node as the selection result, record and output the selection result

     (2) If the type of Broker is not alive, choose to terminate

   2. Cycle the above process until ②is established

   3. The connection path of the output sensor node is the available path for future data communication

   4. Add 1 to the resource state value of all selected nodes to increase congestion

   5. Update the node status in the existing network and record the attribute value of the new entry node

3.4 Network Node Data Communication Algorithm

When a sensor node in the network wants to perform data communication, it first needs to determine the Broker category to which the sensor node belongs, and determine the survival status of the Broker in the category and all nodes on the optional communication path. When the broker and the optional node are in the alive state, the resource state value reflects the current node data communication congestion. According to the principle that the smaller the resource state value, the more idle the node, the greater the probability of being selected, the rational planning of the communication path is realized, to achieve the purpose of rational use of resources and reducing energy consumption. The specific code is shown in Algorithm 2.

Algorithm 2 Network node data communication algorithm

Input: The name of the sensor node that will perform data communication
Output: Sensor node data communication path
    1. Determine the Broker category according to the sensor node name Nodename

    2. Determine whether the Broker in this category is alive

        (1) If the type of Broker survives, start from Nodename, look up the connection status of the node, and get the connection nodes available for selection

        ①If there are connected nodes, judge the survival status of all connected nodes

        A. If the node is alive, record the resource status value of the node

        a. Through the established formula, calculate the sum of the resource state values of all nodes that can be selected and the probability that each node may be selected. The larger the resource state value, the smaller the probability of the node being selected

        b. Determine the node selection through random walk, record and output the selection result

        B. If the node is not alive, then give up the node

        ②If there is no connection node, it will prompt that data transmission is not possible and end the program

        (2) If the type of Broker is not in a surviving state, it will prompt that data transmission is not possible and end the program

    2. Loop the above process until finally connected to Broker0

    3. Output data communication path

    4. Add 1 to the resource state value of all selected nodes to increase congestion

    5. Update the node status in the existing network

4   Experiments and Results

According to the communication algorithm based on node resource status proposed in the third part, experiments are carried out with Fig. 1 as an example to verify the correctness and effectiveness of the algorithm.

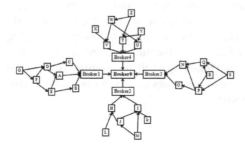

Fig. 1. Experimental verification

In Fig. 1, in addition to the creation node of Broker0, there are four types of Brokers, Broker1, Broker2, Broker3, and Broker4. There are multiple nodes under each Broker to form a directed acyclic graph, which is obtained through data And transmission realizes real-time data acquisition. The node resource states in these four networks are shown in Table 1 respectively.

Table 1. Table captions should be placed above the tables.

Node name	Node category	Resource status value	Node name	Node category	Resource status value
A	Broker1	8	N	Broker3	7
B	Broker1	4	O	Broker3	4
C	Broker1	5	P	Broker3	3
D	Broker1	4	Q	Broker3	3
E	Broker1	3	R	Broker3	1
F	Broker1	2	S	Broker3	1
G	Broker1	1	T	Broker4	3
H	Broker2	4	U	Broker4	4
I	Broker2	5	V	Broker4	4
J	Broker2	2	W	Broker4	2
K	Broker2	1	X	Broker4	1
L	Broker2	1	Y	Broker4	1
M	Broker2	1	Z	Broker4	1

4.1 Experiments and Results of Communication Path Selection Algorithm for New Entry Nodes

For the algorithm in Sect. 3.3, perform experimental verification according to Fig. 1. When the name of the newly added node is tip, for Broker1, there are 6 path schemes, as shown in Table 2; for Broker2, there are 5 path schemes, as shown in Table 3; for Broker3, there are 6 path schemes, as shown in Table 4; for Broker4, there are 6 path schemes, as shown in Table 5.

Taking Broker1 as an example, when all nodes are alive, when a new incoming node wants to join Broker1, the possible output result is shown in Fig. 2.

Under different Broker categories, assuming that the Broker and all nodes are alive, and performing 10,000 experiments respectively, the probability distribution diagram of each path under different categories can be obtained, as shown in Fig. 3. According to the node resource status values in Table 1, it can be found that when the resource status values of the optional nodes have a large difference, the final selection will tend to the path with the smaller resource status value, and when the node resource status values are not much different, probability of the node's communication path selection is similar.

Table 2. Broker1 path selection scheme

Serial number	Path plan	Serial number	Path plan
1	Broker0-Broker1-A-D-F-G	4	Broker0-Broker1-B-E-F-G
2	Broker0-Broker1-A-D-G	5	Broker0-Broker1-C-D-F-G
3	Broker0-Broker1-A-E-F-G	6	Broker0-Broker1-C-D-G

Table 3. Broker2 path selection scheme

Serial number	Path plan	Serial number	Path plan
1	Broker0-Broker2-H-L	4	Broker0-Broker2-I-M
2	Broker0-Broker2-H-J-M	5	Broker0-Broker2-I-K
3	Broker0-Broker2-I-J-M		

Table 4. Broker3 path selection scheme

Serial number	Path plan	Serial number	Path plan
1	Broker0-Broker3-N-P-R	4	Broker0-Broker3-N-Q-S
2	Broker0-Broker3-N-P-S	5	Broker0-Broker3-O-P-R
3	Broker0-Broker3-N-Q-R	6	Broker0-Broker3-O-P-S

Table 5. Broker4 path selection scheme

Serial number	Path plan	Serial number	Path plan
1	Broker0-Broker4-T-Z	4	Broker0-Broker4-U-Y
2	Broker0-Broker4-T-Y	5	Broker0-Broker4-V-W-Z
3	Broker0-Broker4-U-W-Z	6	Broker0-Broker4-V-X

```
Please enter service category,enter 1 to add a new node, enter 2 to send node information:
1
Please enter the number of Broker:
1
Please enter the name of node:
tip
Broker0<---Broker1<---B<---E<---F<---G<---tip
```

Fig. 2. Possible communication path of Broker1 when all nodes are alive

Taking Broker4 as an example, when Broker4 is in the non-survival state, the output result is shown in Fig. 4. If it is assumed that node V is in the non-survival state and the

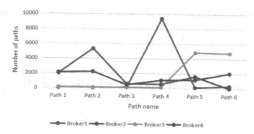

Fig. 3. Results of Broker path selection when all nodes are alive

rest of the nodes are in the alive state, then 100 experiments can be performed to find that there are only four possible communications path, the path containing node V will not appear, and the statistical results are shown in Fig. 5.

```
Please enter service category,enter 1 to add a new node, enter 2 to send node information:
1
Please enter the number of Broker:
4
Broker4is not working, please reselect the service category or try again later!
```

Fig. 4. Output result when Broker4 is not alive

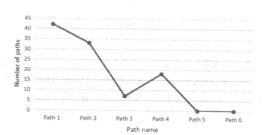

Fig. 5. Output result when node V is not alive

In summary, the new inbound node communication path selection algorithm is correct and effective.

4.2 Network Node Data Communication Algorithm Experiment and Results

For the algorithm in Sect. 3.4, perform experimental verification according to Fig. 1. Taking node J as an example, when node J needs to perform data communication, assuming that all nodes are in a live state, its possible communication path is shown in Fig. 6. When Broker2 is not alive, the output result is shown in Fig. 7.

Taking node F as an example, when node E is in a non-surviving state, the remaining nodes are all alive. After 100 tests, it can be found that among the four alternative communication schemes, only two communication paths can be selected, and no communication path including node E will appear. The statistical results are shown in Fig. 8.

```
Please enter service category,enter 1 to add a new node, enter 2 to send node information:
2
Please enter the name of the node that sends the data:
J
J--->H--->Broker2--->Broker0
```

Fig. 6. Possible communication path of node J in the survival state of all nodes

```
Please enter service category,enter 1 to add a new node, enter 2 to send node information:
2
Please enter the name of the node that sends the data:
J
Broker2is not working, please reselect the service category or try again later!
```

Fig. 7. Output results when Broker2 is not alive

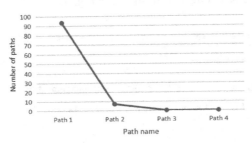

Fig. 8. Output results when node E is not alive

Taking node F as an example, assuming that Broker1 and all nodes are in a survival state, and performing 10,000 experiments, a probability distribution diagram of possible communication paths can be obtained, as shown in Fig. 9.

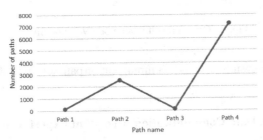

Fig. 9. Probability distribution of the communication path of node F when all nodes are alive

In summary, the data communication algorithm of network nodes is correct and effective.

5 Summary

This paper analyzes the existing problems of data communication in the Internet of Things, and proposes the algorithm design of new entry nodes and data communication, based on the value of node resource status, to realize the selection of possible data communication paths. Through experimental verification, it can be found that the final output results tend to be communication paths with smaller node resource state values, that is, communication paths with relatively idle nodes. Therefore, it can be concluded that the algorithm can make full use of node resources, thereby reducing communication energy consumption and improving transmission efficiency.

Acknowledgments. The authors would like to thank all the anonymous reviewers for their insightful comments. The authors also thank to Professor Zia Tanveer for his kindly review help. This work was supported in part by National Science Foundation of China under No. 61672104, 61170209, 61702570, 61602537, U1509214; Program for New Century Excellent Talents in University No. NCET-13-0676.

References

1. Soni, D., Makwana, A.: A survey on MQTT: a protocol of Internet of Things (IOT). In: International Conference on Telecommunication, Power Analysis and Computing Techniques (ICTPACT - 2017), At Bharath Institute of Higher Education and Research, 173, Agharam Road, Selaiyur, Chennai, India (2017)
2. Stanford-Clark, A., Truong, H.L.: MQTT For Sensor Networks (MQTT-SN) Protocol Specification Version 1.2. (2013)
3. Aziz, B.: A formal model and analysis of an IoT protocol. Ad Hoc Netw. **36**, 49–57 (2016)
4. Coppen, R., Banks, A., Briggs, E., Borgendale, K., Gupta, R.: MQTT Version 5.0 (2019)
5. Haripriya, A.P., Kulothungan, K.. Secure-MQTT: an efficient fuzzy logic-based approach to detect DoS attack in MQTT protocol for internet of things. EURASIP J. Wireless Commun. Network. **2019**(1), 90 (2019)
6. Yu, Z., Hong, H., Xu, G., Zhu, D.: Data encryption transmission algorithm based on MQTT. Comput. Syst. Appl. **28**(10), 178–182 (2019)
7. Elemam, E., Bahaa-Eldin, A.M., Shaker, N.H., Sobh, M.: Formal verification for a PMQTT protocol. Egypt. Inform. J. 2020 (prepublish)
8. Kumar, P., Dezfouli, B.: Implementation and Analysis of QUIC for MQTT. Elsevier B.V. (2018)
9. Rodriguez, A., Kristensen, L.M., Rutle, A.: On modelling and validation of the MQTT IoT protocol for M2M communication (2018)
10. Luzuriaga, J.E., et al.: Improving MQTT data delivery in mobile scenarios: results from a realistic testbed. Mobile Inf. Syst. **2016** (2016)
11. Dinculeană, D., Cheng, X.: Vulnerabilities and limitations of MQTT protocol used between IoT devices. Appl. Sci. **9**(5), 848 (2019)
12. Morales, L.V.V., López-Vizcaíno, M., Iglesias, D.F.: Anomaly detection in IoT: methods, techniques and tools. https://doi.org/10.3390/proceedings2019021004
13. Galán-Jiménez, J., Berrocal, J., Garcia-Alonso, J., Zabal, M.J.: A novel routing scheme for creating opportunistic context-virtual networks in IoT scenarios. Sensors **19**(8), 1875 (2019)
14. Atmoko, R.A., Riantini, R., Hasin, M.K.: IoT real time data acquisition using MQTT protocol. J. Phys. Conf. Series **853**(1) (2017)

15. Kang, Y., Zhong, J., Li, R.: Irrigation system based on message queue telemetry transmission protocol. Sci. Technol. Eng. **20**(08), 3109–3116 (2020)
16. Chouali, S., Boukerche, A., Mostefaoui, A.: Towards a formal analysis of MQtt protocol in the context of communicating vehicles. In: MobiWac 2017: 129–136 a service of Schloss Dagstuhl - Leibniz Center for Informatics homebrowsesearchabout w3c valid html retrieved on 2020-04-28 0
17. Secinti, G., Darian, P.B., Canberk, B., Chowdhury, K.R.: SDNs in the sky: robust end-to-end connectivity for aerial vehicular networks. IEEE Commun. Mag. **56**(1), 16–21 (2018)
18. Xiong, F., Li, A., Wang, H., Tang, L.: An SDN-MQTT based communication system for battlefield UAV swarms. IEEE Commun. Mag. **57**(8), 41–47 (2019)
19. Casadei, R., Fortino, G., Pianini, D., Russo, W., Savaglio, C., Viroli, M.: Modelling and simulation of opportunistic IoT services with aggregate computing. Future Gener. Comput. Syst. **91**, 252–262 (2019)
20. Lindgren, A., Zaitov, A., Mitkov, B.S.: Opportunistic IoT for monitoring of grazing cattle. In: CHANTS 2016: Proceedings of the Eleventh ACM Workshop on Challenged Networks, October 2016, pp. 31–32 (2016)
21. Coutinho, R.W.L., Boukerche, A., Loureiro, A.A.: A novel opportunistic power controlled routing protocol for internet of underwater things. Comput. Commun. **150**, 72–82 (2020)
22. Mukherjee, A., Dey, N., De, D.: EdgeDrone: QoS aware MQTT middleware for mobile edge computing in opportunistic Internet of Drone Things. Comput. Commun. **152**, 93–108 (2020)

Summarization of Coal Mine Accident Reports: A Natural-Language-Processing-Based Approach

Zhigang Zhao[1,2,3], Yang Yang[1,4], Yunlong Wang[1,2,3], Jun Zhang[5], Dezhi Wang[6], and Xiong Luo[1,2,3]($\boxtimes$)

[1] School of Computer and Communication Engineering, University of Science and Technology Beijing, Beijing 100083, China
xluo@ustb.edu.cn
[2] Beijing Key Laboratory of Knowledge Engineering for Materials Science, Beijing 100083, China
[3] Shunde Graduate School, University of Science and Technology Beijing, Foshan 528399, China
[4] School of Computer Science and Engineering, Beihang University, Beijing 100191, China
[5] Science and Technology Division, North China Institute of Science and Technology, Beijing 065201, China
[6] School of Computer Science, North China Institute of Science and Technology, Beijing 065201, China

Abstract. Coal mine production plays an important role in promoting economic development, but the frequent occurrence of coal mine accidents is always a major problem of safety production. Correspondingly, a large number of coal mine accident reports have been generated. These reports detail the causes of safety accidents and the corresponding treatment measures, which have important guidance and reference for the handling of subsequent safety accidents. Nowadays, the analysis efficiency of coal mine accident reports using traditional manual methods is relatively low, and a large amount of valuable information may be not fully exploited and utilized. In response to this deficiency, this paper implements the text mining analysis of coal mine accident reports with the help of currently efficient natural language processing (NLP) technologies, mainly to achieve the text summary of coal mine accident reports. Firstly, after analyzing the overall text framework of the coal mine accident report, the general text structure is presented accordingly. Then, on the basis of it, combining with the TextRank method and Word2vec technique in NLP, the report text structure is optimized, and the report summary library is also obtained autonomously, which helps the staff to deal with accident reports intelligently. The experimental results on the actual text report data verify the effectiveness of the developed method.

Keywords: Natural Language Processing (NLP) · Summarization · Accident report · Coal mine

© Springer Nature Singapore Pte Ltd. 2020
H. Ning and F. Shi (Eds.): CyberDI 2020/CyberLife 2020, CCIS 1329, pp. 103–115, 2020.
https://doi.org/10.1007/978-981-33-4336-8_9

1 Introduction

Coal mines are one of the major energy sources and play an important role in promoting economic development in a country. In the coal mine production, there are also some accidents, which greatly affects the development of the coal resources industry [1, 2]. Then, the government departments have carefully recorded and summarized the major coal mine accidents in the form of reports. Currently, there are a large number of coal mine accident reports. The analysis of coal mine accident reports can identify obvious management problems and hidden dangers of accidents, to effectively make the preventive measures to eliminate the accident in the future. Moreover, according to the accident reports analysis, common features and signs of the accidents may be summarized to spot and cope with the problems in the early stage in future coal mine production. Therefore, it is of great significance to analyze the accident reports.

In the coal mine safety production field, the coal mine accident reports are being generated at a fast scale [3]. Generally, the analysis is based on a handcrafted process, and then humans need to have strong language reading comprehension ability and inductive summarization ability to extract important information from reports. Hence, it is impractical today to implement report analysis tasks totally by manual processing at a great time and expense cost. Actually, the standard coal mine accident reports are with high similarity in their structure and text content [4]. In consideration of it, some methods can be adopted to simplify the processing of coal mine accident reports, thereby extracting valuable information and improving work efficiency. Specifically, it is expected that with the use of a data-driven mechanism, the accident reports could be analyzed more intelligently [5–7].

The past decades have witnessed a rapid advancement of artificial intelligence technologies, which consists of machine learning, data mining, intelligent algorithms, and some other various techniques. Accordingly, it could be expected to use the artificial intelligence techniques, e.g., the natural language processing (NLP), to address those accident reports, considering that there is a great potential of using them in the analysis and reorganization of coal mine accident reports, especially, in China [8]. Hence, an NLP-based approach is proposed here to analyze coal mine accident reports.

In this paper, aiming at the similarities in the content of standard coal mine accident reports, different parts of a report can be extracted through abstracts to generate refined report summaries, using NLP methods. It is helpful for relevant staff to analyze the relationship between coal mine accidents. Through the similarity analysis of the new accident and the existed database, the summary of each part could be reorganized to generate a preliminary accident report template, which enables us to deal with the new accident in combination with the old accident processing plan. Meanwhile, on the basis of analyzing these accident reports, it would be effective to carry out norm rectification and prevent similar accidents.

The main contributions of this paper are as follows:

(1) For the issue of effectively analyzing coal mine accident reports, an NLP-based approach is developed to achieve the summarization of reports, in consideration of the practical organization characteristics of coal mine accident reports.

(2) During the implementation of NLP-based approach, after analyzing the overall structure of some coal mine accident reports from 2010 to 2018 in China, the general text structure of the coal mine accident report is obtained. Then, we sort the sentences using the methods TextRank and Word2vec on the basis of the word-sentence relationship, and optimize the text structure. With the report text structure obtained above, we adjust the acquired sentence weights and generate a report summary database.

This paper is with the following structure. Background information, including coal mine accident reports and text automatic summarization, are presented in Sect. 2. In the next section, the developed summarization approach is described. To verify the NLP-based method, Sect. 4 provides an experimental result in relation to the automatic evaluation performance of summaries. Finally, a conclusion is conducted in Sect. 5.

2 Background

While designing the NLP algorithm, some related information, e.g., the text characteristics, summarization techniques, are introduced in this section.

2.1 The Characteristics of Coal Mine Safety Accident Report

In this paper, we use and analyze about 50 coal mine accident reports in China. The texts and contents of these reports are similar. Although these accident reports differ in the number of first-level headings, their overall meanings are very similar [2, 3]. After carefully integrating the outline of accident reports, it is found that the six first-level headings can be used to represent the overall framework of an accident report.

Here, the text structure template for the accident report is in Fig. 1.

2.2 Text Automatic Summarization

Text automatic summarization is the process of summarizing a document or document corpus through the use of a computer algorithm on the basis of statistics and machine learning techniques, and then we can obtain a summary including all the basic concepts and topics in the original document or corpus [9]. A variety of techniques can be used to design an automated text summarizer. The key idea of all these algorithms is to find a representative subset of the original dataset, where the core elements of the original document or corpus are included in this subset.

Generally speaking, automatic text summarization technologies can be divided into extractive and abstractive algorithms [10]. The former assumes that the text summarization can be attributed to the extraction of some sentences or several words in the text. Thus the text summarization can be transformed into the sort of sentences. The latter generates a summary in accordance with the meaning understanding of the original text content. However, due to the complexity of natural language, the abstractive summarization method performs not well in dealing with long texts [10]. In this paper, automatic

Title
Brief description to the accident. Concern from government. Organization of investigation team according to the regulations. 1. Basic information of the accident unit/enterprise. (1) Enterprise information. (2) Coal mine information. (3) Accident area 2. Accident process and emergency rescue. (1) Process of accident. (2) Accident report and emergency response. (3) Accident handling. 3. Cause of accident. (1) Direct cause. (2) Indirect cause. 4. Characteristics of the accident. 5. Handling suggestions to accident unit/enterprise and persons who are responsible for accident. 6. Prevention measures to accident and rectification suggestions.

Fig. 1. The text structure template for the accident report.

text summarization is achieved through the extractive method, which is simple and easy to be implemented.

In early research, some important text features, e.g., word frequency, word position, are used to extract key sentences to generate extractive summaries. For example, after linearly weighting the four simple sentence features, i.e., word frequency, sentence position, clue words, and title words, the importance of sentences is evaluated [11]. In addition to it, the importance of sentences is also evaluated using external text resources, including thesaurus, background corpus, and knowledge base. In this field, there are two traditional algorithms, i.e., TF-IDF and TextRank. The algorithm TF-IDF introduces external text resources and analyzes the importance of a word from the perspective of the corpus [12]. Specifically, this method combines the term frequency (TF) with the inverse document frequency (IDF) to evaluate the importance of a word.

In [13], the algorithm TextRank was introduced. This algorithm splits text information into text units with a certain granularity, such as words and sentences. They could be denoted as nodes, the similar relationship among those text units could be represented as edges, and then a graph model of the text network is achieved. Hence, the sort for importance is realized by the iterative computing for the above graph. Here, the TextRank model can be represented as a weighted graph $G = (V, E)$, where V is a set of nodes in which node represents a text unit, and E is a set of edges in which edge denotes the relationship between text units. There are n nodes in G, and the score value $W(.)$ of the i-th node v_i ($i = 1, 2, \ldots, n$) is computed as follows [13]:

$$W(v_i) = (1 - d) + d \cdot \sum_{v_j \in I(v_i)} \frac{W(v_j) \cdot w_{ji}}{\sum_{v_k \in O(v_j)} w_{jk}}, \tag{1}$$

where w_{ij} is the weight of nodes v_i and v_j, indicating the similarity between text units. Moreover, $I(v_i)$ represents the set of nodes pointing to v_i, $O(v_j)$ represents the set of nodes to which v_j points, and d is the damping factor whose default value is 0.85.

The performance of algorithm TextRank is usually better than that of the traditional TF-IDF, and it has been widely used in NLP. For examples, a topic model-based summarization, method namely two-tiered model, is proposed through the graph-based TextRank [14], while using the important sentences obtained from TextRank and two-tiered model to extract better summary sentences. In [15], to overcome these shortcomings of only considering the similarities between sentences in the summarization and neglecting information on text structure and context in the use of TextRank, an improved method, called iTextRank, is proposed, while designing a graph through the computation of sentence similarities and the adjustment of weights of nodes by considering statistical and linguistic features. By combining the two characteristics keywords and information types, a method on forestry text key information extraction is proposed using an improved TextRank and clusters filtering [16]. Here, the algorithm TextRank is improved by merging the word features and introducing the edge weights, then the graph model of the text is constructed. Through the comparison with other traditional algorithms such as TF-IDF, the proposed method achieves the satisfactory performance in extracting forestry text keywords.

Furthermore, in the text automatic summarization, there are some algorithms considering the meaning of words and the similarity between words [17]. Word2vec is a set of open-source toolkits for generating word vectors, and it can quickly convert a word into a vector, then the relationship between words can be expressed by calculating the Euclidean distance or angle between word vectors [18]. Through the use of Word2vec, the text automatic summarization algorithm can maintain the semantic relevance between sentences. In [19], a candidate keywords graph is firstly constructed using TextRank, Word2vec is used to calculate the similarity between words as transition probability of nodes' weight, the word score is computed, and then the keyword extraction is implemented. In [20], for the short text comments generated through Twitter, microblogging, and WeChat, Word2vec and Doc2vec are used to improve short-text keyword extraction, where the TextRank model is employed to achieve clustering in a graph.

Motivated by the work mentioned above, this paper uses a combination of the TextRank algorithm and the Word2vec model to achieve a summarization for coal mine accident reports.

3 The Summarization Approach Using Natural-Language-Processing Techniques

In consideration of the practical characteristics of coal mine accident reports, we use TextRank and Word2vec to sort sentences on the basis of word-sentence relationship by means of external information from other background corpus, with the purpose of tackling the relationship between words in a better way, and optimizing the text structure of coal mine accident report. Then, we provide a detailed description for those key parts in the developed summarization method.

3.1 Preprocessing

Here, the background corpus used in this paper is from Chinese Wikipedia [21]. It collects 1.04 million Chinese entries. The entry structure is: {"id": <id>, "url": <url>, "title": <title>, "text": <text>}, where "title" is the caption of entry and "text" is the body, which is wrapped by "\n\n". The corpus here is mainly used to generate values of IDF and train word vectors via Word2vec.

While analyzing the original text, like the operation in [22], we conduct some pre-processing, including word segmentation, word frequency statistics, and removal of stop words. The pseudocode of corpus preprocessing is shown in Fig. 2.

Algorithm: Preprocessing

INPUT: Corpus (Chinese Wikipedia).

OUTPUT: IDF value of corpus and word vector.

1:     Extract the title and text fields from Chinese Wikipedia, and get the corpus C_{origin};
2:     Conduct word segmentation for C_{origin}, and get C_{cut};
3:     Conduct removal of stop words for C_{cut}, and get C;
4:     Train word vector in C, and get word vector set $V_C = v_1, v_2, ...$;
5:     Treat each entry in C as a document, then $C = d_1, d_2, ...$, where d_i (i=1, 2, ...) denotes a document;
6:     **for** each word w_j (j=1, 2, ...) in d_i **do**
7:        Conduct word frequency statistic for w_j;
8:        Calculate IDF value of w_j;
9:     **end for**

Fig. 2. The pseudocode of the preprocessing algorithm.

3.2 Summarization

During the iterative calculation process of summarization, it is mainly based on Tex-tRank, and the more keywords the sentence consists, the greater the weight of the sentence is. Moreover, the higher the frequency of a word in the sentence, the greater the weight of this word is.

Let $S = s_1, s_2, ..., s_m$ be the set of m sentences, where s_i ($i = 1, 2, ..., m$) is a sentence. Let u_i be the weight of sentence s_i, then we can get an m-dimensional vector $u = [u_1, u_2, ..., u_m]$, and generally u_i is set to $1 - d$ initially, where d appears in (1). Let $D = w_1, w_2, ..., w_n$ be the set of n words, where w_j ($j = 1, 2, ..., n$) is a word. Let q_j be the weight of word w_j, and then we can get an n-dimensional vector $q = [q_1, q_2, ..., q_n]$. The initial weight of each word is calculated by the algorithm TF-IDF [12]. After dealing with the word w_j through the use of Word2vec [18], the word vector v_j for w_j is achieved. Furthermore, we can obtain a set of word vectors $V_C = v_1, v_2, ..., v_n$.

The vector x_i of a sentence s_i is denoted as:

$$x_i = \sum_{w_j \in D_i} v_j \cdot q_j, \tag{2}$$

where D_i represents a set of those words contained in the sentence s_i.

This paper uses cosine angle of two sentence vectors to calculate the similarity between sentences as follows:

$$f(x_i, x_j) = \frac{x_i \cdot x_j}{\|x_i\| \cdot \|x_j\|}, \tag{3}$$

where $f(.,.)$ denotes a similarity value and x_i, x_j are two arbitrary sentence vectors in set V_C.

On the basis of graph sorting technique in the TextRank algorithm, in this paper, the sentence is regarded as a node, and a set of nodes is generated as V. Meanwhile, the similarity between sentences in (3) is regarded as the edge weight between nodes, and a set of edge weights is generated as E. Then, we can obtain the adjacency matrix of a graph $G = (V, E)$ as follows:

$$A(G) = \begin{bmatrix} 0 & a_{12} & \cdots & a_{1m} \\ a_{21} & 0 & \cdots & a_{2m} \\ \vdots & \vdots & \ddots & \vdots \\ a_{m1} & a_{m2} & \cdots & 0 \end{bmatrix}, \tag{4}$$

where a_{ij} is the similarity between sentences s_i and s_j, and $a_{ij} = f(x_i, x_j)$.

In the algorithm TextRank [13], the importance of a node depends on the number of adjacent nodes pointing to it and the importance of those adjacent nodes. Then, according to (1), the importance of a sentence node can be computed by:

$$u_i = (1 - d) + d \cdot \sum_{s_j \in I(s_i)} \frac{u_j \cdot a_{ji}}{\sum_{s_k \in O(s_j)} a_{jk}}, \tag{5}$$

where $d = 0.85$ is the damping factor, $I(s_i)$ denotes the set of nodes pointing to the sentence node s_i, and $O(s_j)$ denotes the set of nodes to which the sentence node s_j points. Here, u_i is the weight of the sentence node s_i, and a_{ij} is the similarity between the i-th sentence s_i and the j-th sentence s_j. In (5), the weight of the current sentence is calculated on the basis of the similarity with other sentences and the weights of those sentences. Such iterative calculations are performed on each sentence until convergence, then the final weight of each sentence can be achieved. When the difference between the former and the latter weight of each sentence is less than the threshold value of 0.0001, we consider it as convergence [13].

Additionally, with the weights of sentences in (5), we can update the weight of the j-th word ($j = 1, 2, \ldots, m$) by:

$$q_j = \frac{\sum_{i=1}^{m} p_{ij} u_i}{\sum_{i=1}^{m} p_{ij}}, \tag{6}$$

where p_{ij} represents the TF value of the word w_j in the sentence s_i and m denotes the number of sentences.

Using (6), the weight of each sentence can be recalculated by [23]:

$$u_i' = \frac{\sum_{j=1}^{n} p_{ij} q_j}{\sum_{j=1}^{n} p_{ij}}, \tag{7}$$

where n denotes the number of words in sentence s_i.

Through the combination of (5) and (7), a modified sentence weight is achieved by [23]:

$$u_i'' = \gamma \times u_i + (1 - \gamma) \times u_i', \tag{8}$$

where $\gamma \in (0, 1)$ is a weight factor.

Here, we perform the iterative computation for the $\boldsymbol{u''} = \left[u_1'', u_2'', \ldots, u_m''\right]$ using (5), (6), (7), and (8). When the difference of iteratively computed $\boldsymbol{u''}$ is less than a specified threshold value, the computation is stopped, and the converged $\boldsymbol{u''}$ is taken as the final sentence weight vector. Hence, all sentences can be sorted on the basis of the final sentence weight. Then, the summarization is accordingly achieved. The above summarization process is named as Algorithm S.

Then, since the sorted sentences are generally based on the word-sentence relationship and algorithm TextRank, and the original text structure is not considered. It means that the title sentence and some special sentences in the original text are not fully used. For the coal mine accident report, the overall framework is relatively obvious. If we only sort sentences ignoring the impact of the overall framework in the accident report, the sentence weights generated by using the above TextRank-based algorithm may be lower, in consideration of the fact that the title sentence and some special sentences are generally with a short length. Hence, the summarization performance of Algorithm S may be unsatisfactory. In response to such limitation, the title sentences in the coal mine accident reports are accordingly added into the sentence set of text automatic summarization directly. In so doing, we can achieve the summary results which are very close to that of manual extraction. The modified summarization process is named as Algorithm S^*.

Specifically, motivated by the work in [13, 24], the pseudocode of Algorithm S^* used to generate a summary database for the coal mine accident report is listed in Fig. 3.

4 Experimental Results and Discussion

In this paper, 50 coal mine accident reports in China are used to test the algorithm performance. These reports are similar in style and content [25]. Although these accident reports differ in the number of primary headings, their overall meaning is very similar.

4.1 Metric

Currently, the performance of text automatic summarization is evaluated through a recall-oriented understudy for the gisting evaluation (ROUGE) method [26]. In the NLP field, ROUGE is used to evaluate the performance of automatic summarization and machine translation software. If the manual scoring is used to evaluate the text automatic summary results, it may be unreliable to a certain degree of subjectivity. The ROUGE evaluates the performance of automatic text summaries by counting the number of co-occurrences of n-gram semantic units from statistical machine summaries and manual reference summaries. Through the experimental test, the evaluation results of this method have a good correlation with the results of manual evaluation, and are more objective.

Algorithm S^*: Summarization for the coal mine accident report

INPUT: Coal mine accident report $R=r_1, r_2, ...$

OUTPUT: A summary library with 5 parts in Fig. 1,

denoted as $Y=Sum_1, Sum_2, Sum_3, Sum_4, Sum_6$.

1:    **for** r_i $(i=1, 2, ...)$ in **R do**

2:       Conduct the preprocessing for corpus r_i using the algorithm in Fig. 2;

3:       Conduct sentence segmentation for r_i, and get $r_i=s_{i1}, s_{i2}, ...,$

       in which mark title sentence;

4:       Use (5)~(8) to compute the weight of sentences $s_{i1}, s_{i2}, ...$ in r_i, and

       get weight set $U_i=u_{i1}, u_{i2}, ...;$

5:       **for** sentence s' of the 3rd part in r_i **do**

                           // Address the third part of the accident report separately

6:         **for** word w' in 'ImWords' **do**   // 'ImWords' represents a list of important word

7:           **if** w' in s' **then**

8:              $u' \leftarrow u' \times 1.3;$ // u' is the weight of sentence s'

9:           **end if**

10:         **end for**

11:      **end for**

12:      **for** $k = 1 \rightarrow 6$ **do**   // Address those parts in report

13:       **if** $k = 5$ **then**   // Do not address the 5th part

14:         continue

15:       **end if**

16:       Sort the sentences in the k-th part of r_i according to the weight set U_i;

17:       Put the title sentence in the k-th part of r_i into Sum_k;

18:       $l_{max} \leftarrow$ Length(the k-th part of r_i)$\times$ 0.4;   // Use 40% of each part as a summary

19:       $l \leftarrow l_{max} -$ Length(the title sentence in Sum_k);

20:       **for** s' in the k-th part of the sorted r_i **do**

21:         **if** $l < l_{max}$ **then**

22:         Put s' into Sum_k;

23:         $l \leftarrow l -$ Length(s');

24:        **end if**

25:       **end for**

26:      **end for**

27:   **end for**

Fig. 3. The pseudocode of the summarization algorithm for the coal mine accident report.

It is noted that while using ROUGE, the evaluation object of automatic text summarization mainly focuses on English text, and there are not too many results on Chinese text. Here, we use ROUGE as a metric to test the algorithm performance in handling coal mine accident reports with Chinese text.

In this paper, the metric is denoted as ROUGE-n, which represents the n-gram recall between an automatic summary and a set of reference summaries, and it is defined as [26]:

$$ROUGE - n = \frac{\sum_{\mathcal{H} \in R_S} \sum_{ngram \in \mathcal{H}} \widetilde{Count(ngram)}}{\sum_{\mathcal{H} \in R_S} \sum_{ngram \in \mathcal{H}} Count(ngram)} \qquad (9)$$

where $n\overline{gram}$ is the n-gram, n is the length of $n\overline{gram}$, $Count(\widetilde{n\overline{gram}})$ represents the maximum number of n-grams co-occurring between an automatic summary and a set of reference summaries, $Count(n\overline{gram})$ represents the number of $n\overline{gram}$, and $\mathbf{R}_S$ denotes the set of reference summaries.

4.2 Impact of the Sentence Weight Factor

In (8), $\gamma \in (0, 1)$ as the sentence weight factor, affects the final value of $\mathbf{u}''$. Then, we provide an analysis on how to set γ to achieve the fast convergence for $\mathbf{u}''$. We take the number of iterations to get the final $\mathbf{u}''$ as the measurement. The fewer iterations, the better the γ is.

By varying the value of γ from 0 to 1 with a step size 0.05, we record the corresponded number of iterations to get the final $\mathbf{u}''$. The result is shown in Fig. 4. It can be found that when γ is about 0.5, the number of iterations is the lowest and the convergence is the fastest. Therefore, in this paper, $\gamma = 0.5$.

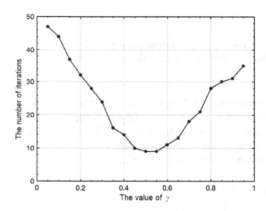

Fig. 4. Impact of the weight factor γ on the convergence speed.

4.3 Performance Evaluation

In this paper, considering TextRank is more common text summarization approach in coal mine safety, here TextRank is used as the baseline. For the text structure of coal mine accident reports in China with 6 parts as shown in Fig. 1, the summary is manually extracted for each part, and the result is used as a reference summary. After performing the traditional TextRank [13] and Algorithms S and $S^\star$ in Sect. 3 on coal mine accident reports, the summarization performance is evaluated through the ROUGE-1 and ROUGE-2, which are the metric as $n = 1$ and 2 in (9). The results are shown in Tables 1 and 2.

It is obvious that the satisfactory performance is achieved by using Algorithms S and $S^\star$. Specifically, since the text structure characteristics of coal mine accident reports are

Table 1. Evaluation result of ROUGE-1.

	Traditional algorithm TextRank	Algorithm S	Algorithm $S^\star$
The 1st part	0.454	0.510	0.535
The 2nd part	0.460	0.531	0.592
The 3rd part	0.423	0.532	0.698
The 4th part	0.812	0.812	0.812
The 6th part	0.436	0.560	0.560
Full text	0.441	0.529	0.564

Table 2. Evaluation result of ROUGE-2.

	Traditional algorithm TextRank	Algorithm S	Algorithm $S^\star$
The 1st part	0.334	0.432	0.440
The 2nd part	0.351	0.453	0.472
The 3rd part	0.332	0.443	0.531
The 4th part	0.803	0.803	0.803
The 6th part	0.354	0.449	0.449
Full text	0.342	0.434	0.460

incorporated into the design of summarization algorithm, Algorithms S and $S^\star$ perform better than the traditional TextRank, furthermore Algorithms $S^\star$ performs better than Algorithms S.

5 Conclusion

This paper mainly focuses on the text automatic summarization technology for the coal mine accident report, while presenting an NLP-based structured summary generation approach. Through the comprehensive analysis on the overall structure of the coal mine accident reports from 2010 to 2018 in China, the general text structure of the coal mine accident report is obtained. Then, we combine with the TextRank method and Word2vec technique on the basis of word-sentence relationship, to sort the sentences, and to optimize the text structure. Furthermore, for the report text structure obtained above, we adjust the acquired sentence weights and achieve a report summary database. Evaluation results verify that the NLP-based approach achieves a good performance. While using the developed summarization method, it enables the staff to analyze accidents efficiently.

Acknowledgement. This work was supported in part by the National Key Research and Development Program of China under Grant 2018YFC0808306, by the Scientific and Technological

Innovation Foundation of Shunde Graduate School, USTB, under Grant BK19BF006, and by the Fundamental Research Funds for the University of Science and Technology Beijing under Grant FRF-BD-19-012A.

References

1. Akgun, M.: Coal mine accidents. Turk. Thorac. J. **16**, S1–S2 (2015)
2. Wang, X., Meng, F.: Statistical analysis of large accidents in China's coal mines in 2016. Nat. Hazards **92**(1), 311–325 (2018)
3. Zhang, J., Xu, K., Reniers, G., You, G.: Statistical analysis the characteristics of extraordinarily severe coal mine accidents (ESCMAs) in China from 1950 to 2018. Process Saf. Environ. Prot. **133**, 332–340 (2020)
4. Cao, Y.: Analysis of accident source and preventive measures in local coal mine. In: The 4th International Conference on Advances in Energy Resources and Environment Engineering, Chengdu, 032082, Institute of Physics Publishing (2019)
5. Kumar, P., Gupta, S., Gunda, Y.R.: Estimation of human error rate in underground coal mines through retrospective analysis of mining accident reports and some error reduction strategies. Saf. Sci. **123**, 104555 (2020)
6. Liu, M.: Analysis of Influencing Factors and Risk Prediction of Aviation Safety Accident Report Based on Text Mining. Anhui Jianzhu University, Hefei (2019)
7. Huang, Y.: Research Based on Natural Language Processing for Risk of Construction Accident Reports. Huazhong University of Science & Technology, Wuhan (2019)
8. Qiao, W., Li, X., Liu, Q.: Systemic approaches to incident analysis in coal mines: comparison of the STAMP, FRAM and "2-4" models. Resour. Policy **63**, 101453 (2019)
9. Gambhir, M., Gupta, V.: Recent automatic text summarization techniques: a survey. Artif. Intell. Rev. **47**(1), 1–66 (2017)
10. Hahn, U., Mani, I.: The challenges of automatic summarization. Computer **33**(11), 29 (2000)
11. Edmundson, H.P.: New methods in automatic extracting. J. ACM **16**(2), 264–285 (1969)
12. Kim, D., Seo, D., Cho, S., Kang, P.: Multi-co-training for document classification using various document representations: TF–IDF, LDA, and Doc2Vec. Inf. Sci. **477**, 15–29 (2019)
13. Mallick, C., Das, A.K., Dutta, M., Das, A.K., Sarkar, A.: Graph-based text summarization using modified TextRank. In: Nayak, J., Abraham, A., Krishna, B.Murali, Chandra Sekhar, G.T., Das, A.K. (eds.) Soft Computing in Data Analytics. AISC, vol. 758, pp. 137–146. Springer, Singapore (2019). https://doi.org/10.1007/978-981-13-0514-6_14
14. Akhtar, N., Beg, M.M.S., Javed, H.: TextRank enhanced topic model for query focussed text summarization. In: The 12th International Conference on Contemporary Computing, Noida, 8844939. IEEE (2019)
15. Yu, S., Su, J., Li, P., Wang, H.: Towards high performance text mining: a TextRank-based method for automatic text summarization. Int. J. Grid High Perform. Comput. **8**(2), 58–75 (2016)
16. Chen, Z., Li, Y., Xu, F., Feng, G., Shi, D., Cui, X.: Key information extraction of forestry text based on TextRank and clusters filtering. Trans. Chin. Soc. Agric. Mach. **51**(5), 207–214 (2020)
17. Altmami, N.I., Menai, M.B.: Automatic summarization of scientific articles: A survey. J. King Saud Univ. Comput. Inf. Sci. (2020). https://doi.org/10.1016/j.jksuci.2020.04.020
18. Tomas Mikolov. Word2vec project. https://code.google.com/p/Word2vec/. Accessed 3 Aug 2020

19. Wen, Y., Yuan, H., Zhang, P.: Research on keyword extraction based on Word2Vec weighted TextRank. In: The 2nd IEEE International Conference on Computer and Communications, Chengdu, pp. 2109–2113. IEEE (2016)
20. Li, J., Huang, G., Fan, C., Sun, Z., Zhu, H.: Key word extraction for short text via word2vec, doc2vec, and textrank. Turk. J. Electr. Eng. Comput. Sci. **27**(3), 1794–1805 (2019)
21. Chinese Wikipedia. https://github.com/brightmart/nlp_chinese_corpus. Accessed 3 Aug 2020
22. Jones, K.S.: A statistical interpretation of term specificity and its application in retrieval. J. Doc. **60**(5), 493–502 (2004)
23. Xu, C., Liu, D.: Chinese text summarization algorithm based on Word2vec. In: International Conference on Control Engineering and Artificial Intelligence, Boracay, 012006. Institute of Physics Publishing (2018)
24. Li, F., Huang, J.Z., Li, Z.J., Yang, W.M.: Automatic summarization method of news texts using keywords expansion. J. Front. Comput. Sci. Technol. **10**(3), 372–380 (2016)
25. Wang, J.J.: Research on the Standard of Investigative Report in Coal Mine Accident. Taiyuan University of Science and Technology, Taiyuan (2016)
26. Iinuma, S., Nanba, H., Takezawa, T.: Automatic Summarization of Multiple Travel Blog Entries Focusing on Travelers' Behavior. In: Stangl, B., Pesonen, J. (eds.) Information and Communication Technologies in Tourism 2018, pp. 129–142. Springer, Cham (2018). https://doi.org/10.1007/978-3-319-72923-7_11

The College Student Credit Evaluation Based on Characteristic Data

Ying Xu[1,2], Yuejia Gu[3], Jiangpan Wang[1,2(✉)], and Xin Su[4]

[1] Shanghai Lixin University of Accounting and
Finance, Shanghai 201209, People's Republic of China
pan623813@163.com
[2] School of Financial Technology, Shanghai Lixin University of Accounting and Finance,
Shanghai 201209, People's Republic of China
[3] School of Public Finance and Administration, Shanghai Lixin University of Accounting and
Finance, Shanghai 201209, People's Republic of China
[4] College of IoT Engineering, Hohai University, Changzhou 213022, People's Republic of China

Abstract. The increasing demand for high-tech talents has placed additional significance on the academic achievement for college students. Consequent to this demand, academic misconducts have become widespread in college and university. It has become apparent that an evaluation of college students' academic and social integrity is necessary in face of such circumstance. This paper focuses on providing a new characteristic data to detailing the college students' credit evaluation, using data sourced from academic related behavior such as trends in occupying library seating. Analytic Hierarchy Process (AHP) algorithm is the model chosen to evaluate student credit. As a supplement, an Area Under Curve (AUC) evaluation model was produced for a comparison against the Sesame Credit Score of Alipay to produce a 52.7% accuracy reading of our model. The results show that the credit score of academic behavior data is consistent with the credit score generated from the economic data used in the Sesame system. For that reason, our method can provide an alternative means for estimating economic credit rating as academic behavior data of college students can be evaluated to serve as a reference. This study supports the Education Office and the universities in their effort to improve the moral correctness of college students through rewarding academic honesty and punishment of dishonest behavior. Furthermore, the model proposed in this study can be invaluable to the field of psychological education, as data generated can serve as basis for future analysis in psychological counseling.

Keywords: College students' behavior in school · Credit evaluation system · AHP · AUC

1 Introduction

The "credit rating" system aims to prevent moral hazard and mitigate adverse selection. The rating object can be evaluated by professionals in accordance to pre-determined scoring standards, which results in a comprehensive understanding of the rating object's

© Springer Nature Singapore Pte Ltd. 2020
H. Ning and F. Shi (Eds.): CyberDI 2020/CyberLife 2020, CCIS 1329, pp. 116–130, 2020.
https://doi.org/10.1007/978-981-33-4336-8_10

credit situation that can be expressed in the term of words or symbols. An example of information asymmetry is observed in personal current credit analysis. The difficulty of reviewing and tracking private loan information forces bank and other information users to use personal historical credit information as a alternative. In situations where high degree of information asymmetry exists in the credit market and the phenomenon of bad debts is difficult to quantify, the "efficiency funnel" effect would be observed. Behavior data for college students are often scarce as they generally start off socially stagnant, which results in an incomplete credit history. On the other hand, college students have a wealth of data in academic activities. Therefore, it is unreasonable to adopt a "one size fits all" approach to the credit investigation of the graduate students. If these data presented in academic activities can be used for credit analysis, it would be the supplement to the lack of behavior data for the credit information of college students. These data can be further utilized after the graduation when students enter the workforce.

In 2017, the "National University Integrity Culture Education Alliance" and "Shanghai integrity culture research center" [1] were established in Shanghai Lixin Accounting and Finance College. According to the mission statement, "Education Alliance" aims to establish a platform for honest cultural exchange, cooperation and sharing between colleges and universities, integrate "scientific research, education, teaching and cultural communication", as well as promote honest cultural education in Colleges and Universities. The "Research Center" focuses on major issues in the fields of integrity culture and credit systems, and prioritize on solving contemporary and complex Issues such as the establishment of regional credit indicators, credit rating and credit risk management. Based on this, this paper conducts a field survey of more than 500 students from a Shanghai university. The collected data of their academic behavior was examined, and upon further analysis, a set of credit subsystem was put forth for these college students.

1.1 Previous Studies

The problem of credit risk is apparent among college students. Credit risk is mainly reflected in three aspects: schooling, social and economics. The credit risk from schooling is mainly present in the form of academic fraud and cheating during examinations [2]. The social aspect is mainly reflected in theft [3], and the economic aspect is mainly in three of loans [4]. Nowadays, Colleges and Universities in China have issued policies to mitigate academic misconduct, such as termination of misbehaved professors, canceling graduation examination, reducing the rate of reexamination of graduation thesis, etc. At the same time, college students are facing greater employment pressure, which drive students to improve their academic capability. In the past decade, accompanying the rapid development of China's economy is a lack of credit systems which has caused serious problems. In 2002, Guo et al. [5] used Analytic Hierarchy Process (AHP) to measure the economic credit of college students mainly using data from their natural background, student status management, daily income and expenditure, student loans and other aspects. It provided a quantitative way to measure the credit of the university students in China. Lina et al. [6] used genetic neural network to evaluate the personal credit of college students, and improved the traditional neural network algorithm by reducing the training time; it also served to provide technical support for both the credit risk avoidance of college students and the implementation of the national student loan policy. In July 2016, the issuance of the youth credit system construction plan [7] and the survey report on the credit status of Chinese college students in 2017 [8] raised a discussion on college students' credit. Due to the disconnect between college students and social finance, newly-employed college graduates experienced restrictions in their use of financial services. Jiong Mu et al. [9] used Random Forest (RF) algorithm to evaluate college students' credit, taking into account "basic personal situation", "school situation" and "economic situation". Ahn et al. [10] took a hierarchical multiple regression analysis and a regulatory factor analysis to explore the impact of psychological and cognitive biases on College Students' credit.

1.2   Brief Introduction to AHP

The Analytic Hierarchy Process (AHP) is a decision-making method that decomposes the elements related to the total amount of decisions into levels, such as goals, criteria and plans, then carries out qualitative and quantitative analysis on this basis.

AHP (Analytic Hierarchy Process), is a general process that is applicable and flexible. It has been extensively studied and widely used, since its first proposal by Saaty [11]. Lin [12] combined AHP and DEA (Data Envelopment Analysis) model to evaluate the local economic development progress in China. In Yaraghi's [13] paper, they proposed a simulation approach to compare the results of AHP with Monte Carlo analytic hierarchy process (MCAHP) under different levels of uncertainty, and showed that when pairwise comparisons are less than 0.24, the performance of AHP is not statistically different from the performance of MCAHP. This shows that the performance of AHP is still valuable in most application. Most of the up-to-date researches on College Students' credit are based on the approval and issuance of student loans, whereas we focus on the learning attitude and study integrity behavior of college students. We pay full attention to college students' behavior in school, especially their academic behavior, and try to establish a picture of students' credit to provide new insight for the whole process of education, namely "San Quan" Education [14]. This paper combines the 5C element theory of index credit system mentioned by Chen [15] and the index set up by Guo et al. [5] for college students' AHP rating, and selects some indexes and models suitable for college students according to the relevant standards of financial industry. Meanwhile, because the financial/credit data of College students is difficult to obtain and the training samples are very limited, the final network model is not stable. To solve the problem of network stability, additional data need to be collected and the model should be trained with samples for a long time. However, AHP does not need as many training data sets as neural network, and previous works have used AHP to measure college students' credit. Therefore, we have chosen the traditional AHP as the main model algorithm for stability. In this paper, we use the Area Under Curve (AUC) method to verify the credibility of the final credit score.

2   Method

To achieve the target (Z), we need to divide the target into several criteria (C) as shown in Fig. 1. According to the correlation degree of each criterion and target, we weight each criterion which is obtained by comparing the two criteria. Finally, by multiplying the weight, we can obtain the final score of each. The higher they get, the more credible they are.

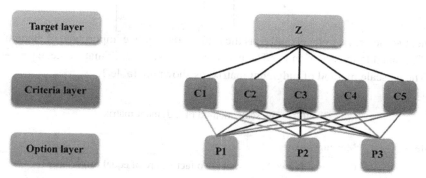

Fig. 1. Weight each criterion according to the correlation degree of each criterion and target

2.1 Consistency Test

In this paper, judgment matrices are constructed according to each secondary index by the 1–9 proportional scale method. We take judgment matrix **A** as an example. We design three judgment matrices including matrix **A**, matrix **B**, and matrix **C**. Judgment matrix **A** is the relative importance among Academic integrity (AI), Life integrity (LI), and Student development bank business (SD). The Judgment Matrix **B** is the relative importance among five parts, including Cheating in exams (CE), Violation of discipline within school (VD), Truancy (TR), Overdue return of books (OB), and Overdue return of equipment (OE). Judgment matrix **C** is the relative importance among 7 parts, including Timely return of property (TP), Steal property (SP), Violation of laws and regulations (VR), Didn't attend the lecture as scheduled (DS), occupy seat in library (OI), and Failure to return the umbrella on time (FT), Bicycles are placed at will (BW). The Judgment Matrix **D** is the relative importance between Arrears of tuition or accommodation (AA), and times of entering school and issuing blacklist (TB).

Here we give an example to judge the consistency of the hierarchical matrix. The method of constructing the judgment matrix in the AHP method is the consistent matrix method, that is, instead of comparing all the factors together, but pairwise comparison. In order to improve the accuracy, the relative scale is used to reduce the difficulty of comparing the factors with different properties.

$$\text{Judgment matrices } E = (a_{ij})_{n*n} = \begin{bmatrix} F_k & E_1 & E_2 & & E_n \\ E_1 & e_{11} & e_{12} & \cdots & e_{1n} \\ E_2 & e_{21} & e_{22} & & e_{2n} \\ & \vdots & \vdots & \ddots & \vdots \\ E_n & e_{n1} & e_{n1} & \cdots & e_{nn} \end{bmatrix}, \text{ } F_k \text{ is the } K^{th} \text{ criterion}$$

element at the previous level, and e_{ij} is the ratio of the relative importance of element E_i and E_j related to the criterion F_k. The matrix E is the symmetric matrix, i.e. $e_{ij} = \frac{1}{e_{ij}}$.

The e_{ij} scale method of judgment matrix, as shown in Table 1.

Table 1. The scale method of judgment matrix

Scale	Meaning
1	Compared to two factors, the two factors are of equal importance
3	Compared to two factors, one factor is slightly more important than the other
5	Compared to two factors, one factor is significantly more important than the other
7	Compared to two factors, one factor is more important than the other
9	Compared to two factors, one factor is extremely important than the other
2, 4, 6, 8	The median of the above two adjacent judgments
Countdown	Judgment of comparison of factor i with factor j, as e_{ij}; then judgment of comparison of factor j with i, as $\frac{1}{e_{ij}}$

2.2 Weight Value and Corresponding Consistency Ratio CR Value

(i) Taking matrix E as an example, calculate the continued product of each row of elements in judgment matrix E:

$$M_i = \prod_{j=1}^{n} e_{ij}, \quad i, j = 1, 2, \ldots, n \tag{1}$$

(ii) Calculate the Nth root of M_i:

$$W_i' = \sqrt[n]{M_i} \tag{2}$$

(iii) Vector $W_i' = \left[W_1', W_2', \ldots, W_n' \right]^T$ normalization:

$$W_i' = \frac{W_i'}{\sum_{i=1}^{n} W_i'} \tag{3}$$

So $W = [W_1, W_2, \ldots, W_n]^T$ is the feature vector.

(iv) Calculate the maximum feature vector of the matrix λ_{max}:

$$\lambda_{max} = \sum_{i=1}^{n} \frac{(PW)}{nW_i} \tag{4}$$

(v) Consistency check:

Consistency index: $CI = \frac{\lambda_{max} - n}{n-1}$.

Consistency ratio: $CR = \frac{CI}{RI}$.

It is generally considered that when the consistency ratio $CR < 0.1$, the degree of inconsistency of E is considered to be within the allowable range, and there is satisfactory consistency. The normalized eigenvector can be used as a weight vector, otherwise, the pair comparison matrix E must be reconstructed, and the relative importance of element e_{ij} should be adjusted (Table 2).

Table 2. Mean random consistency index

n	0	1	2	3	4	5	6	7	8	9	10
RI	0	0	0.58	0.9	1.12	1.24	1.32	1.41	1.45	1.49	1.51

3 Experiment Result

3.1 Experiment Data

The questionnaire is designed according to the pre-set index classification table, which is mainly divided into five categories. In addition to the pre-set indicators, namely, academic integrity, life integrity and academic distribution business, the economic behavior analysis and open-ended issues are added to analyze the main motivation of student loans and the causes of students' academic dishonesty. In order to facilitate the respondents to answer and improve the integrity of their answers, the questionnaire was designed with objective options except for the cost of living, sesame credit score and monthly loan limit.

According to the needs of credit investigation, accounting, finance and other indus-tries have higher requirements on the credit level of employees. Therefore, the project team selects the college students of Shanghai Lixin University of Accounting and Finance as samples to carry out a sampling survey. A total of 547 questionnaires were collected by the project team, and those with large area of continuous options (more than 50% of the content is continuous option) and large area of blank content (more than 50% of the content is blank) were regarded as waste volumes. After screening, there were 6 waste volumes, with an effective rate of 98.9%.

3.2 Set Criteria

Our overall goal Z is to estimate college student's credit. We have designed a two-layer of criteria system C1 and C2, as shown in in Fig. 1. The layer C1 consists of three parts: Academic integrity (AI), Life integrity (LI), and Student development bank business (SD), the other layer consists of 14 parts, as depicted in Fig. 2. P stands for an opinion group, which refers to the credit score of each student in the group.

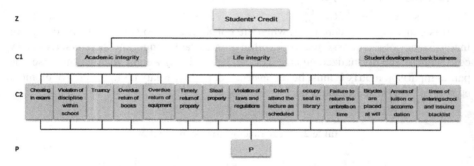

Fig. 2. Hierarchical structure

The selection of indicators refers to the code of conduct for students in China's higher education. Article 5 of the code of conduct indicates that students should abide by aca-demic integrity and should not cheat or plagiarize. In addition, in the general provisions, the rules require that college students should not violate the law and discipline. In terms of lectures and library seats, we refer to the rules and regulations of Shanghai Lixin Institute of accounting and finance. What's different from the previous research is that we don't involve personal learning achievement and gender characteristics indicators, because we don't think these indicators are the factors that affect integrity.

3.3 Criteria Layer Judgment Matrix and Weight Calculation

The Delphi method is used to determine the weights of the indicators in this study. We invite 6 students to do it separately, and ask them to score each indicator. Then all the scoring questionnaires are subjected to the weight calculation and consistency test in the AHP method. The weight and average score of the indicator are finally calculated to determine judgment matrix **A**.

Table 3. Decision hierarchy for students' credit

Criteria	Sub-criteria	Index score	Index type
Academic integrity (AI)	Cheating in exams (CE)	Actual value filling in the questionnaire	Minimal type
	Violation of discipline within school (VD)	Actual value filling in the questionnaire	Minimal type
	Truancy (TR)	Actual value filling in the questionnaire	Minimal type
	Overdue return of books (OB)	Actual value filling in the questionnaire	Minimal type
	Overdue return of equipment (OE)	Actual value filling in the questionnaire	Minimal type
Life integrity (LI)	Timely return of property (TP)	Every time: 5 points, 80% cases: 4 points, 50% cases: 3 points, 30% cases: 2 points, No: 1 point	Maximal type
	Steal property (SP)	No: 5 points, yes: 1 point	Bool type
	Violation of laws and regulations (VR)	No: 5 points, yes: 1 point	Bool type
	Didn't attend the lecture as scheduled (DS)	0 time: 5 points, 1–2 times: 4 points, 3–5 times: 3 points, 6–10 times: 2 points, more than 10 times: 1 point	Minimal type
	Occupy seat in library (OI)	0 time: 5 points, 1–3 times: 4 points, 5-10:3 points, 10–20 times: 2 points, more than 20 times: 1 point	Minimal type
	Failure to return the umbrella on time (FT)	Return within one day each time: 5 points, Once or twice more than a day, but also returned: 4 points, More than three times over a day, but also returned: 3 points, Non return: 2 points	Minimal type

(*continued*)

Table 3. (*continued*)

Criteria	Sub-criteria	Index score	Index type
	Bicycles are placed at will (BW)	Park in the designated parking lot and shed every time: 5 points, 80% of the cases will be parked in designated parking spots and sheds: 4 points, 50% will park in designated parking spots and sheds: 3 points, No attention has been paid to the parking place, almost every time they park at the door of dormitory and teaching building at will: 2 points	Minimal type
Student development bank business (SD)	Arrears of tuition or accommodation (AA)	0 time: 5 points, 1 time: 3 points, 2 times: 1 point	Minimal type
	times of entering school and issuing blacklist (TB)	0 time: 5 points, 1 time: 3 points, 2 times: 1 point	Minimal type

	AI	LI	SD
AI	1	8/7	8/9
LI	7/8	1	7/9
SD	9/8	9/7	1

$$A = \begin{bmatrix} 1 & 1.143 & 0.889 \\ 0.875 & 1 & 0.778 \\ 1.125 & 1.286 & 1 \end{bmatrix} \tag{6}$$

Based on the above formula (1)–(4), we get the consistency check: $\lambda_{max} = 3.003$, $CI = 1.2632e - 04$, $RI = 0.58, CR = 2.1780e - 04$.

After calculation, the weight vector is $Q = \begin{bmatrix} 0.3333 & 0.2917 & 0.3750 \end{bmatrix}$

3.4 Program Layer Judgment Matrix and Weight Calculation

The Judgment Matrix **B** is the relative importance among five parts, including Cheating in exams (CE), Violation of discipline within school (VD), Truancy (TR), Overdue return of books (OB), and Overdue return of equipment (OE). The judgment matrix of the program layer of Academic integrity is obtained as follows:

	CE	VD	TR	OB	OE
CE	1	1/2	4/2	9/2	9/2
VD	2/1	1	4/1	9/1	9/1
TR	2/4	1/4	1	9/4	9/4
OB	2/9	1/9	4/9	1	9/9
OE	2/9	1/9	4/9	9/9	1

$$B = \begin{bmatrix} 1 & 0.5 & 2 & 4.5 & 4.5 \\ 2 & 1 & 4 & 9 & 9 \\ 0.5 & 0.25 & 1 & 2.25 & 2.25 \\ 0.22 & 0.11 & 0.44 & 1 & 1 \\ 0.22 & 0.11 & 0.44 & 1 & 1 \end{bmatrix} \tag{7}$$

Based on the above formula (1)–(4), we get the consistency check: $\lambda_{max} = 4.988$, $CI = -0.0030, RI = 1.24, CR = -0.0027 < 0.1$. The matrix **B** passed the consistency test.

After calculation, the weight vector is $Q = [0.254\ 0.507\ 0.127\ 0.056]$

Judgment matrix **C** is the relative importance among 7 parts, including Timely return of property (TP), Steal property (SP), Violation of laws and regulations (VR), Didn't attend the lecture as scheduled (DS), occupy seat in library (OI), and Failure to return the umbrella on time (FT), Bicycles are placed at will (BW). The judgment matrix of the program layer of Life integrity is obtained as follows:

	TP	SP	VR	OS	OI	FI	BW
TP	1	1/2	3/8	5/4	3	5/2	5/4
SP	2	1	3/4	5/2	6	5	5/2
VR	8/3	4/3	1	10/3	8/1	20/3	10/3
OS	4/5	2/5	3/10	1	12/5	2	1
OI	1/3	1/6	1/8	5/12	1	5/6	5/12
FI	2/5	1/5	3/20	1/2	6/5	1	1/2
BW	4/5	2/5	3/10	1	12/5	2	1

$$C = \begin{bmatrix} 1 & 0.5 & 0.375 & 1.25 & 3 & 2.5 & 1.25 \\ 2 & 1 & 0.75 & 2.5 & 6 & 5 & 2.5 \\ 2.67 & 1.33 & 1 & 3.33 & 8 & 7 & 3.33 \\ 0.8 & 0.4 & 0.3 & 1 & 2.4 & 2 & 1 \\ 0.33 & 0.167 & 0.125 & 0.416 & 1 & 0.833 & 0.417 \\ 0.4 & 0.2 & 0.143 & 0.5 & 1.2 & 1 & 0.5 \\ 0.8 & 0.4 & 0.3 & 1 & 2.4 & 2 & 1 \end{bmatrix} \tag{8}$$

Based on the above formula (1)–(4), we get the consistency check: λ_{max} = 6.999, CI = −0.000232, RI = 1.32, CR = −0.000176 < 0.1, the matrix **C** passed the consistency test. After calculation, the weight vector is Q = [0.125 0.250 0.334 0.099 0.042 0.050 0.099].

The Judgment Matrix **D** is the relative importance between Arrears of tuition or accommodation (AA), and times of entering school and issuing blacklist (TB). The judgment matrix of the program layer of Business in Student Development Bank is obtained as follows:

	AA	TB
AA	1	10/17
TB	17/10	1

$$D = \begin{bmatrix} 1 & 0.588 \\ 1.7 & 1 \end{bmatrix} \tag{9}$$

Based on the above formula (1)–(4), we get the consistency check: λ_{max} = 1.999, CI = −2.0002e − 04, RI = 0, CR = −Inf < 0.1, the matrix D passed the consistency test.

After calculation, the weight vector is Q = [0.370 0.630].

Analysis results from the above judgment matrix, we can see that the CR of all judgment matrices are less than 0.1, that is, they all pass the consistency test, and the structure of the single-order hierarchy has satisfactory consistency. According to the above calculations, the corresponding criterion-level weights × plan-level weights can be used to obtain comprehensive weights. The weights of College student credit evaluation index system are summarized in Table 3.

The consistency check of the hierarchical total ordering is as follows:

$$CI = -0.003 \times 0.3333 + (-0.0029) \times 0.2917 + (-2.002e^{-04}) \times 0.375 \approx 0.0019 < 0.1,$$
$$RI = 1.24 \times 0.3333 + 1.32 \times 0.2917 + 0 \times 0.375 \approx 0.798,$$
$$CR = \frac{CI}{RI} = 0.0024 < 0.1.$$

AHP test under the criteria of academic integrity, life integrity and business in student development bank (Table 4).

Notes: Under the test, we get the weight of every sub-criteria, and rank it by ourselves. Then through the consideration of weight of criteria, we get the total weight, and the total sort.

Table 4. Selection of standard splitting threshold and parameter

Criteria		Sub-criteria		Singal-sort	Total weight	Total-sort
Criteria	Weight (%) (Ranking)	Factors	Weight (%)			
Academic integrity	0.3333 (2)	B1 Times of cheating in examinations	0.2537	3	0.08455821	6
		B2 Times of criticism	0.5074	2	0.16911642	3
		B3 Total class hours of truancy in one year	0.1268	4	0.04226244	8
		B4.2 Times of overdue book returns	0.0560	5	0.0186648	12
		B5.2 Times of overdue equipment returns	0.560	1	0.186648	2
Life integrity	0.2917 (3)	C2 Times of giving items to the owner	0.1252	3	0.03652084	9
		C3 Whether to steal property without permission	0.2504	2	0.07304168	7
		C4 Punishment for violation of laws and regulations	0.3338	1	0.09736946	5
		C5 Times of absent from the lecture	0.0995	4	0.02902415	10
		C6 Times of occupying seats in the library	0.0419	7	0.01222223	14
		C7 Practice of using integrity umbrella	0.0497	6	0.01449749	13

(*continued*)

Table 4. (*continued*)

Criteria		Sub-criteria		Singal-sort	Total weight	Total-sort
Criteria	Weight (%) (Ranking)	Factors	Weight (%)			
		C8 Practice after using bicycle	0.0995	5	0.02902415	11
Business in Student Development Bank	0.3750 (1)	D1 Times of tuition fees or accommodation fees in arrears	0.3703	2	0.1388625	4
		D3 Number of students on the student development bank blacklist	0.6297	1	0.2361375	1

4 Validity

Comparative method is adopted in this experiment. The above algorithm is compared with the high-quality object called Sesame Credit Score from Alipay.

The data is divided into two categories: benchmark set and non-benchmark set, where the benchmark set is generally recognized as Sesame Credit Score (credit score). We conduct 'it' times independent comparison experiment: we select a group of objects (i, j) from the benchmark set in random order, and mark sesame credit score as credit score(i), credit score(j), and mark a = credit score(i) − credit score(j). In addition, the corresponding objects(i, j) in the non-benchmark set were identified, which were marked as our score(i) and our score(j), and b = our score(i) − our score(j). Then the relationship between the values of a and b was compared. If a and b had the same sign marked as n_1, and if a = b was marked as n_2, the AUC value was calculated as follows:

$$AUC\_score = \frac{n_1 + 0.5 * n_2}{it} \tag{10}$$

Figure 3 shows the AUC score between our method and Sesame Credit Score from Alipay as different length k from 50 to 500. We can see that the AUC score is from 52.5% to 53%, the average accuracy is 52.7%.

It can be seen from the figure that the credit score calculated by AHP method is in good agreement with the Sesame Credit Score.

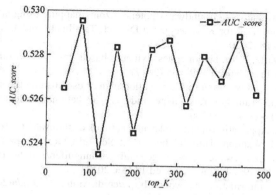

Fig. 3. The AUC score of our method and Sesame Credit Score from Alipay as different length k from 50 to 500

5   Conclusion

College students are indispensable subjects to personal credit investigation. Consequent of their unique consumption habits and lack of behavior data, credit evaluation of college students has always been a perplexing financial problem.

Based on the data of college students' academic behavior, this paper constructs a credit evaluation for college students through AHP algorithm. Quantitative evaluation was applied to examine students from three general aspects of academic integrity, the social integrity and economic integrity. Insufficiencies of the conventional traditional society credit investigation method was supplemented through this quantitative evaluation. Finally, in order to verify the effectiveness of our algorithm, comparison was made against the Sesame Credit Score by AUC algorithm. Results have shown that our method generates an accuracy of 52.7%. The credit rating of college students' credit investigation has practical significance and wide application. This paper aims to contribute to the college students' credit. The emerging advances in information technology (e.g. the facial recognition system) can further support the credit rating system by providing functions such as recognition. Regardless of the location of the inquiry, the system will record the related activities of college students, which can be widely applied in circumstances such as job, and loan application and so forth.

Acknowledgements. This work is partially supported by Funds for the construction of the application-oriented undergraduate pilot majors in Shanghai universities-financial engineering majors (financial science and technology) (Nos. B1-12-2801-19-001Z).

References

1. Western Network. http://news.cnwest.com/content/2017-05/22/content_1490989.html. Accessed 22 May 2017
2. Yang, J., Vargas, L.G., Jin, X., Zhou, L.: Quality credit evaluation in the internet company: a system based on the analytic hierarchy process. J. Bus. Econ. Manage. **21**(2), 344–372 (2020)

3. Saranya, T., Saravanan, S.: Groundwater potential zone mapping using analytical hierarchy process (AHP) and GIS for Kancheepuram District, Tamilnadu, India. Model. Earth Syst. Environ. **6**(6), 1–18 (2020)
4. Tatum, H., Schwartz, B.M.: Honor codes: evidence based strategies for improving academic integrity. Theory Pract. **56**(2), 129–135 (2017)
5. Guo, J., Zhao, X.: Study on the implementation plan of establishing the system of personal credit inquiry and evaluation for college students with national student loan. High. Educ. China 2003(024).003, 47–49 (2003)
6. Lina, L., Jian, H.: Application of artificial neural network on the evaluation of college student's personal credit. J. Shandong Univ. Technol. (Nat. Sci. Ed.) **22**(5), 77–80 (2008)
7. China credit. https://www.creditchina.gov.cn/biaozhunguifan/zonghexingbiaozhunguifan/201712/t20171214_99924.html. Accessed 14 Dec 2017
8. China financial information network. http://credit.xinhua08.com/a/20170811/1720718.shtml?f=arelated. Accessed 11 Aug 2017
9. Mu, J., Xu, L., Pu, H.: Study on college student credit evaluation and prediction based on RF algorithm. J. Digit. Inf. Manage. **12**(1), 26–30 (2014)
10. Ahn, S.-Y., Kuo,Y.-H., Serido, J., Shim, S.: Direct and interaction effects of cognitive bias and anxiety on credit misuse among U.S. college students. Family Enviorn. Res. **56**(5), 447–460 (2018)
11. Yan, K., Zhu, J., He, T.: The deficiency and improvement of AHP in multi-objective decision-making process. Stat. Decis. Making **237**, 10–11 (2007)
12. Lin, M.-I., Lee, Y.-D., Ho, T.-N.: Applying integrated DEA/AHP to evaluate the economic performance of local governments in China. Eur. J. Oper. Res. **209**, 129–140 (2011). https://doi.org/10.1016/j.ejor.2010.08.006
13. Yaraghi, N., Tabesh, P., Guan, P., Zhuang, J.: Comparison of AHP and Monte Carlo AHP under different levels of uncertainty. IEEE Trans. Eng. Manage. **62**(1), 122–132 (2015)
14. Ministry of Education of the People's Republic of China. http://www.moe.gov.cn/s78/A12/moe_2154/201903/t20190308_372733.html. Accessed July 2019
15. Chen, Y.: Several theoretical problems of establishing credit rating index system. Res. Finan. Issues **201**(8), 3–8 (2000)

Research on Human Pose Estimation and Object Detection in the Field of Unmanned Retail

Leiming Liu, Linghao Lin, and Jiangyun Li[✉]

University of Science and Technology Beijing, Beijing, China
leejy@ustb.edu.cn

Abstract. The key part of unmanned retail is how to judge who bought which product. To solve the problems, we propose a method that combines human pose estimation and commodity detection algorithm based on deep learning. To process videos in real-time, we apply depth separable convolution to modify the human pose estimation algorithm, reduce the size of convolution kernel, and fuse multi-stage information. To detect commodities, we construct a commodity detection dataset to train the object detection model. The modified pose estimation algorithm is used to identify key points of the left and right wrists of the human body, and the object detection algorithm recognizes products existing in the current image, we calculate the distance between key points and products, using this value to determine whether the customer has purchased a certain product. As a result, we tested the proposed pipeline in real scenarios, it can determine whether the user purchased the product. This method which only uses computer vision for judgment is convenient to deploy and further development of unmanned retail. Research results have been applied to brick-and-mortar stores.

Keywords: Unmanned retail · Human pose estimation · Object detection

1 Introduction

Unmanned retail, such as automatic vending machines, unmanned supermarkets, and other automatic vending systems, are widely used in daily life due to their non-personal contact characteristics. Especially during the period of COVID-19 (Corona Virus Disease 2019), the way of life and work without personal contact greatly reduced the risk of infection, further promote the development of the unmanned retail sector. From Amazon Go to Ali's Coffee, Internet leaders continue to increase investment in the unmanned retail industry [1]. At present, the common unmanned retail solutions mainly include three types, the first is based on two-dimensional code; The second is to use RFID(Radio Frequency Identification) technology; The third is utilizing computer vision and deep learning technology to build unmanned retail solutions.

Unmanned retail stores built with two-dimensional code, using product QR codes or barcodes to complete the identification and management of goods, users complete the billing self-service. This approach is similar to traditional retailing, but there will be a low cost of commodity management. Unmanned retail stores built with RFID

© Springer Nature Singapore Pte Ltd. 2020
H. Ning and F. Shi (Eds.): CyberDI 2020/CyberLife 2020, CCIS 1329, pp. 131–141, 2020.
https://doi.org/10.1007/978-981-33-4336-8_11

using RFID tags attached to the products to complete the identification of goods. This approach requires attaching an RFID tag to each product and recording product-related information, resulting in high maintenance costs. Unlike the two scenarios mentioned above, unmanned retail stores based on computer vision and deep learning technologies, using machine vision to judge the user's shopping behavior and leveraging biometric technology to complete payment. There is no store clerk monitoring and duplicate actions such as cash registers throughout the shopping process, reducing direct contact, and greatly simplifying the shopping process. So this approach is the main development direction of unmanned retail stores.

Benefit from the rapid development of big data and deep learning technologies in recent years, the use of deep learning to solve image problems has become a key research area, such as object detection algorithm can accurately identify the location and class information of objects in the image; the human body key points present in the image can be identified by the human pose estimation algorithm; the ability to accurately split the specified objects through semantic segmentation algorithms and the use of GAN (Generative Adversarial Networks) to achieve the style migration of images, etc. These provide conditions for the realization of an unmanned retail system based on computer vision and deep learning technology (the third type of solution).

In the process of implementing the third type of program, a very important part is how to determine which user has purchased which type of goods. Aiming at this problem, we combine the human pose estimation algorithm OpenPose [2] based on deep learning and object detection algorithm YOLO [3] to solve it. Besides, we modify the pose estimation model based on OpenPose to make it have better real-time performance.

Overall Process: First, we identify all key points of the human body in the picture through the pose estimation algorithm, and connect key points belonging to the same person according to the physiological structure, record key points of the left and right wrist parts; At the same time, using object detection algorithm to detect products in the picture. Second, we calculate the Euclidean distance between the key point of the wrist and the position of the product, using it to determine whether the customer has purchased the product.

The structure of this paper is organized as follows: In Sect. 2, we describe what human pose estimation and object detection are. Section 3 discusses how to build models and reports results in Sect. 4. Finally, the paper is concluded in Sect. 4.

2   Algorithm Introduction

2.1   Human Pose Estimation

Human pose estimation [4] refers to using a pose estimation algorithm to detect key points of the human body in an image or video and connect key points belonging to the same human body according to the physiological structure, thereby forming a complete human body posture. At present, multi-person human pose estimation algorithms based on deep learning are divided into two categories: Top-Down and Bottom-Up.

Top-Down. The top-down human pose estimation algorithm is divided into two steps. First, the object detection algorithm is used to identify the possible human targets in the image and cut them out. Then they are sent to the single-person pose estimation model to obtain key points of the human body. This method converts multi-person pose estimation problem into multiple single-person pose estimation problems, which is relatively simple to implement. However, this method relies heavily on the accuracy and speed of the object detection algorithm and when there are too many objects in the input image, the processing time is greatly increased. To reduce the dependence of human pose estimation on the accuracy of object detection, Hao-Shu Fang et al. proposed the SSTN(Symmetric Spatial Transformer Network) [5], which can adjust the position of human object detection boxes to improve the accuracy of keypoint detection. In terms of data processing, Junjie Huang et al. proposed a UDP (Unbiased Data Processing) method [6] to problem that the result obtained by flipping the image is not aligned with the original image and the use of encoder-decoder structures has large statistical errors.

Bottom-Up. The bottom-up method first detects all key points of the human body that may exist in the picture and then connects key points belonging to the same person to completes human pose estimation. This method directly gets the coordinates of key points and does not rely on the target detection algorithm, so inference speed is less affected by the number of people. However, there are two main problems with this kind of method. First, the bottom-up method needs to directly detect all key points in the entire image, and the size of the human body is not fixed, so it is necessary to solve the multi-scale problem. Second, what method should be taken to correctly connect them after getting key points. To solve the first problem, Bowen Cheng et al. proposed HigherHRNet [7], which integrates multiple levels of features in the model to improve the positioning accuracy of the key points for small targets. For the second difficulty, Zhe Cao et al. proposed PAF (Part Affinity Fields) [2] which can encode the connection relationship between key points.

2.2 Object Detection

The task of object detection [8] is to find out location and class information of objects in the image. The current mainstream algorithms fall into two categories: One-Stage and Two-Stage.

The One-Stage method uses CNN (Convolutional Neural Network) to extract image features and directly get the target's position and class information. The speed is faster.

YOLO adopts a single CNN network to process the image. This network divides the image into regions and predicts bounding boxes and probabilities for each region. Wei Liu et al. propose a single shot multi-box detector [9] which takes a pyramid-like structure to predict the object category and location on different scales feature maps. Tsung-Yi Lin et al. believe that one-state is inferior to two-stage because of the imbalance in the number of positive and negative samples. So they proposed the Focal Loss [10] which is modified based on the standard cross-entropy loss. This loss function reduces the weight of easy samples so that the model focuses more on difficult samples during training.

The Two-Stage method is divided into two steps. Firstly, it will generate a series of proposal boxes, then classify and regress the candidate boxes. This kind of method is more accurate. R. Girshick et al. proposed R-CNN [11] which first uses the selective search method to generate a series of candidate boxes, feed these boxes into a CNN model, finally regress coordinate values and use SVM (Support Vector Machine) [12] to classify. For RCNN, the selective search method generates about two thousand candidate boxes, and every box feed into CNN to get a fixed-length vector, this operation consumes a lot of time. To solve this problem, R. Girshick proposed Fast R-CNN [13] which uses CNN to extract features of the entire picture and then utilize ROI pooling to get a fixed-length vector. But the processing speed is still slow due to the selective search method. Shaoqing Ren et al. proposed RPN (Region Proposal Network) [14] and integrates the steps of generating candidate boxes into CNN, so the model can be trained end-to-end and the inference speed has been greatly improved. In the field of video object detection, Sara Beery et al. propose an attention-based approach that allows model, Context R-CNN [15], to index into a long term memory bank constructed on a per-camera basis and aggregate contextual features from other frames to boost object detection performance on the current frame.

3   Model

3.1   The Human Pose Estimation Model

Since the Top-Down human pose estimation method relies heavily on the performance of object detection algorithm and is greatly affected by the number of people, we take the more mature OpenPose in the Bottom-Up method as the main framework. Based on it, the network structure is modified to reduce the number of parameters and meet real-time requirements of actual deployment.

The main structure of OpenPose is shown in Fig. 1, including feature extraction network VGG [16], human key points branch and the PAF (Part Affinity Fields) branch. The feature extraction network VGG performs operations such as convolution, pooling, normalization and nonlinear mapping on the input image to extract hidden features of the image. The human key points branch which is used to predict key points of the human body that may exist in the picture firstly applies three 3×3 and two 1×1 convolutions to refine the output of the backbone, and then stacks identical blocks to continuously adjust the predicted key points position; The PAF branch which is responsible for predicting the correlation information between various key points is similar to the human key points branch structure, stacking multiple identical blocks to continuously refine prediction accuracy of PAF. The L2 loss function is used to calculate loss value during training. In order to avoid the disappearance of gradient and enable the network to better converge, the intermediate supervision [17] method is used to calculate the loss of each module, and final loss f is obtained after addition.

$$f = \sum_{n=1}^{6} (f_1^t + f_2^t) \tag{1}$$

After obtaining human key points and PAF information, the Hungarian algorithm is used to match key points, connect these belonging to the same person.

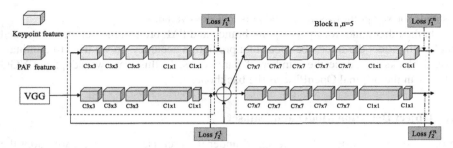

Fig. 1. OpenPose network structure

The original version of OpenPose takes 0.073 s to process an image on TITAN RTX GPU, which is slow. In order to deploy the model in practice, we need to speed up algorithm inference. So we adjusted the backbone, key point branch and PAF branch according to the above architecture.

On the one hand, considering that the depth separable convolution used by MobileNetV2 [18] can greatly reduce the number of parameters, it is used as a backbone, and all ordinary convolutions in the key point branch and PAF branch are replaced with depth separable convolution. Besides, to improve network performance, we fusion low-level visual features and high-level semantic features. The network structure is shown in Fig. 2. There is a feature extraction network MobileNetV2, we take features of the fifth layer, seventh layer and fourteenth layer, then we concatenate these feature maps. For the key point branch and PAF branch, we adopt depth separable convolution and replace 7×7 kernel size with 3×3 which can reduce the number of parameters by 9 times. For the loss function, due to the PAF branch predicts key point connection information of each point in the feature map, this information is a two-dimensional vector, but the output of the key point branch is single-valued information, so in order to balance the loss value of two branches, a weighted loss function is used. The weight of the key points branch's loss is doubled. The loss function is defined as follows:

$$f = \sum_{n=1}^{6} (2 \times f_1^t + f_2^t) \tag{2}$$

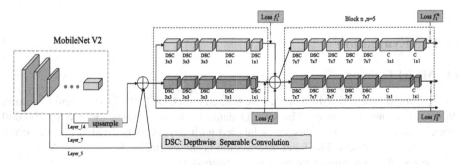

Fig. 2. Use MobileNetV2 to modify OpenPose

f_1 stands for key point loss value and f_2 is PAF loss value.

On the other hand, for the key point branch and PAF branch, the number of stacked blocks will affect the inference speed and prediction accuracy, so we tried to eliminate several blocks to reduce the number of parameters. In this way, we adopt the VGG network in the original OpenPose as the backbone.

3.2   Object Detection Model and Dataset

In order to have a faster inference speed under the premise of accuracy, we adopt the YOLO object detection algorithm. YOLO is a one-stage detection algorithm that directly generates the position of object, balance accuracy and speed.

To train the object detection model, a training data set needs to be constructed. We use three cameras to collect information on the appearance of products. To increase the diversity of data, each category is collected multiple images from different angles, different backgrounds and different light conditions. We collected 6796 pictures using 10 categories of products. Then we used the labelImg tool to label collected data. As shown in Fig. 3, here are three types of product images in the dataset. Figure 4 shows the picture marked with the labelImg. After finishing labeling, we get labels of each picture, which records the upper left corner, lower right corner and category information of the target. Finally, we converted these labels to the VOC dataset format and feed it into YOLO for training.

Fig. 3. Pictures were taken with cameras

4   The Evaluation

4.1   Model Training

For the human pose estimation model, we trained it on COCO2017 (Microsoft Common Objects in Context) dataset. The COCO dataset which contains more than 200,000 images and 250,000 person instances labeled with keypoints is divided into the train, validation, and test sets. The label information is shown in Fig. 5.

The specific experimental details are as follows:

Fig. 4. Annotated pictures

Fig. 5. Human keypoints in COCO

When using the network shown in Fig. 1, we load OpenPose pre-training weights, discard the last block, refines model parameters, the initial learning rate is 0.0005, and stop after 25 iterations.

When using the network shown in Fig. 2, we load MobileNetV2 pre-training weights, the initial learning rate is 0.001, the batch size is 32, the training process takes 69 h, and we stop training after 135 iterations.

We use 4 NVIDIA TITAN RTX GPUs for processing the above solutions, and the input images are resized to 432×368 resolution. The experimental results are shown in Table 1. OpenPose represents the unchanged version; OpenPose-1Block represents remove the last Block; DCS + OpenPose represents the OpenPose modified with depth separable convolution which is shown in Fig. 2.

In Table 1, removing the last Block of OpenPose can reduce the number of parameters, inference time is reduced by 0.0012 s, but the acceleration effect is not significant; DCS + OpenPose has greatly reduced the number of convolution parameters due to the use of deep separable convolutions, and reasoning time is shortened by 51.97% compared with the original version. In terms of accuracy, since in actual application scenarios, the human body occupies most of the camera field of view when it is necessary to determine whether a customer purchases a product, so large-scale objects are considered.

Table 1. Model performance comparison.

Model	AP^{large}(%)	FLOPs	Time(s)
OpenPose	50.33	104623076	0.0737
OpenPose-1Block	46.98	87053398	0.0725
DCS + OpenPose	42.21	23886946	0.0354

The accuracy of DCS + OpenPose is reduced by 8.12% when detecting large targets. There are two main reasons. On the one hand, the depth separable convolution weakens the information between channels. As shown in Fig. 6, the traditional convolution operation will fuse information of all channels at the same time. However, for the depth separable convolution, each channel of the convolution kernel is only responsible for one dimension of the input feature as shown in Fig. 7.

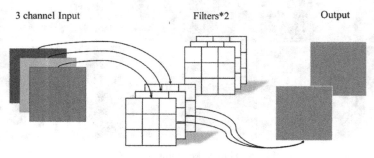

Fig. 6. Conventional convolution operation

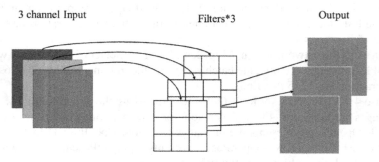

Fig. 7. The first step of deep separable convolution

On the other hand, replacing 7×7 convolution with 3×3 shrinking the receptive field which is not conducive to capturing more information.

The actual test results are shown in Fig. 8, the left side is OpenPose output, the right side is DCS + OpenPose output, we can see that in the case of no occlusion, the results of these two methods are broadly in line; When the human body is blocked, some key points generated by DCS + OpenPose have a certain offset, but due to the improvement of DCS + OpenPose inference speed, more images can be processed per second, and there is a high probability that no occlusion can be captured. Therefore, relative to a decrease in accuracy, the improvement in processing speed is of greater significance for practical applications.

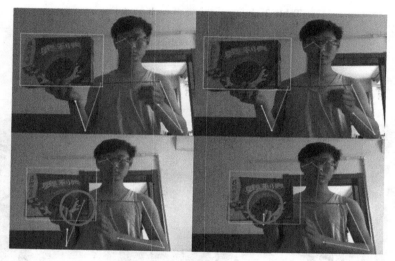

Fig. 8. Picture of test results

For the object detection model, we use a self-built product dataset to train the YOLOv3 model and apply some data enhancement methods to increase the robustness of the model, such as random rotation, adjustment of contrast and brightness, etc. We resize input images into 416×416 resolution, the initial learning rate is 0.001, the batch size is 32, the training process takes 20 h on 2080Ti GPU.

4.2 Pipeline

First, we use human body pose estimation algorithm to detect possible key points of a customer in the camera field of view, select key points of the left and right wrists as P_L (X_L, Y_L) and $P_R (X_R, Y_R)$, then use object detection algorithm to detect products that may exist in the field of view, and record its center position (X_i, Y_i). Finally, we use Eq. 3 and 4 to calculate the Euclidean distance between product and P_L, P_R respectively. If the distance is less than threshold, the customer corresponding to this key point is considered to have purchased the product; If there are multiple distances less than the threshold at the same time, take the minimum distance. We use 1280×720 resolution images to test, and the threshold distance is set to 240 pixels.

$$dL = \sqrt{(X_L - X_i)^2 + (Y_L - Y_i)^2} \tag{3}$$

$$dR = \sqrt{(X_R - X_i)^2 + (Y_R - Y_i)^2} \qquad (4)$$

The inference time of the overall scheme on NVIDIA TITAN RTX GPU is shown in Table 2 and the test results are shown in Fig. 9.

Table 2. Inference time of each module.

Module	Pose estimation	Object detection	Overall
Time(s)	0.0335	0.0198	0.0533

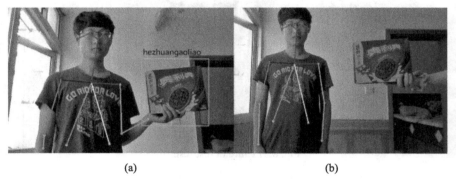

(a)   (b)

Fig. 9. Test results of the pipeline

We can see that our proposed pipeline process one image takes 0.0533 s in Table 2. So it can be deployed in practice.

As shown in Fig. 9(a), the distance between the center point of a product and key point of the left wrist is 166 pixels and the value is less than threshold which is 240, so we draw the product location and information to indicate that the customer has purchased this product; as shown in Fig. 9(b), the distance is 475 pixels greater than threshold, so no processing is done.

5 Conclusion

In this paper, we proposed a method to judge what goods the user has purchased in an unmanned retail scene. First, we built a product data set to realize product detection. Second, we apply depth separable convolution to speed up the inference speed of the human pose estimation model. Finally, we combine human pose estimation and object detection algorithms to determine whether the user purchased the product. It was shown that the pipeline can successfully judge customer purchase behavior in real-time. Compared with traditional methods, our method does not require auxiliary equipment (such as RFID, etc.). It is convenient to deploy in-store. However, it costs a lot of money to deploy this method on GPU servers. So the future work can be carried out around how to optimize algorithm so that it can be deployed on edge devices(such as NVIDIA Jetson Nano or T × 2, etc.).

References

1. Zeng, X.: Artificial intelligence promotes the rise of unmanned retail. Enterp. Manage. **11** (2017)
2. Cao, Z., Hidalgo, G., Simon, T., Wei, S.-E., Sheikh, Y.: OpenPose: realtime multi-person 2D pose estimation using part affinity fields. arXiv preprint arXiv:1812.08008(2018)
3. Redmon, J., Farhadi, A.: YOLO9000: better, faster, stronger. In: Proceedings of the IEEE Conference on Computer Vision and Pattern Recognition, pp. 7263–7271 (2017)
4. Munea, T.L., Jembre, Y.Z., Weldegebriel, H.T., Chen, L., Huang, C., Yang, C.: The progress of human pose estimation: a survey and taxonomy of models applied in 2D human pose estimation. IEEE Access **8**, 133330–133348 (2020). https://doi.org/10.1109/ACCESS.2020. 3010248
5. Fang, H.-S., Xie, S., Tai, Y.-W., Lu, C.: RMPE: regional multi-person pose estimation. In: The IEEE International Conference on Computer Vision (ICCV), 2.K, October 2017
6. Huang, J., Zhu, Z., Guo, F., Huang, G.: The devil is in the details: delving into unbiased data processing for human pose estimation. ArXiv, abs/1911.07524 (2019)
7. Cheng, B., Xiao, B., Wang, J., Shi, H., Huang, T., Zhang, L.: HigherHRNet: scale-aware representation learning for bottom-up human pose estimation. In: 2020 IEEE/CVF Conference on Computer Vision and Pattern Recognition (CVPR), pp. 5385–5394 (2020)
8. Nisa, S.U., Imran, M.: A critical review of object detection using convolution neural network. In: 2019 2nd International Conference on Communication, Computing and Digital systems (C-CODE), Islamabad, Pakistan, pp. 154–159 (2019). https://doi.org/10.1109/c-code.2019. 8681010
9. Liu, W., et al.: SSD: single shot multibox detector. In: Leibe, B., Matas, J., Sebe, N., Welling, M. (eds.) ECCV 2016. LNCS, vol. 9905, pp. 21–37. Springer, Cham (2016). https://doi.org/ 10.1007/978-3-319-46448-0_2
10. Lin, T.-Y., Goyal, P., Girshick, R., He, K., Dollar, P.: Focal loss for dense object detection. arXiv preprint arXiv:1708.02002, 8 July 2017
11. Girshick, R., Donahue, J., Darrell, T., Malik, J.: Rich feature hierarchies for accurate object detection and semantic segmentation. In: CVPR (2014)
12. Chen, P.H., Lin, C.J., Schölkopf, B.: A tutorial on ν-support vector machines. Appl. Stoch. Models. Bus. Ind. **21**, 111–136 (2005)
13. Girshick, R.: Fast R-CNN. In: 2015 IEEE International Conference on Computer Vision (ICCV), Santiago, pp. 1440–1448 (2015). https://doi.org/10.1109/iccv.2015.169
14. Ren, S., He, K., Girshick, R., Sun, J.: Faster R-CNN: towards real-time object detection with region proposal networks. In: NIPS (2015)
15. Beery, S., Wu, G., Rathod, V., Votel, R., Huang, J.: Context R-CNN: long term temporal context for per-camera object detection. In: CVPR (2020)
16. Simonyan, K., Zisserman, A.: Very deep convolutional networks for large-scale image recognition. In: ICLR (2015)
17. Li, C., Zia, M.Z., Tran, Q., Yu, X., Hager, G.D., Chandraker, M.: Deep supervision with intermediate concepts. IEEE Trans. Pattern Anal. Mach. Intell. **41**(8), 1828–1843 (2019). https://doi.org/10.1109/tpami.2018.2863285
18. Sandler, M., Howard, A., Zhu, M., Zhmoginov, A. Chen, L.-C.: MobileNetV2: inverted residuals and linear bottlenecks. In: CVPR (2018)

Edge Computing-Based Solution and Framework for Software-Defined Industrial Intelligent Control in Industrial Internet of Things

Pengfei Hu[1,2(✉)] and Chunming He[3]

[1] Research Institute of HollySys Group Co., Ltd., Beijing 100176, China
hupengfei@hollysys.com
[2] Beijing HollySys Co., Ltd., Beijing 100176, China
[3] HollySys Group Co., Ltd., Beijing 100176, China

Abstract. The Industrial Internet of Things (IIoT) enables intelligent interaction and automated collaboration among industrial production factors (i.e., human, machine, thing, method and environment) to improve productivity and intelligent level of factory. The industrial intelligent control system is the basis for realizing IIoT. It can enable industrial production with the abilities of autonomous decision-making and system autonomy. As an extension and expansion of the industrial cloud platform capabilities, edge computing can support industrial intelligent control with low-latency, high-reliability, and high-security edge intelligent services. Combined with the ideas and technologies of edge computing, software definition and Cyber-Physical System (CPS), we propose the solution and framework of software-defined industrial intelligent control (SDIIC) to realize intelligent control based on edge computing from two levels of software and hardware. At the software level, we propose the scheme of industrial intelligent control oriented software-defined edge computing (SDEC) platform to realize the intelligent and flexible management and autonomous coordination of edge devices. At the hardware level, the architecture and key technologies of the software-defined edge controller are proposed. The software-defined virtual controller with differentiated control and computing capabilities is implemented on the general standardized hardware resources. It can support both real-time industrial control and non-real-time edge computing task processing. The SDEC platform and the software-defined edge controller enable the SDIIC solution to realize industrial system autonomy and intelligent control.

Keywords: Industrial Internet of Things (IIoT) · Edge computing · Industrial intelligent control · Software definition · Edge controller

1 Introduction

The development of Industrial Internet of Things (IIoT) and Cyber-Physical System (CPS) has enabled the manufacturing industry to transform and upgrade to digital, networked, and intelligent, and move towards the industry 4.0 era [1]. By building the

© Springer Nature Singapore Pte Ltd. 2020
H. Ning and F. Shi (Eds.): CyberDI 2020/CyberLife 2020, CCIS 1329, pp. 142–153, 2020.
https://doi.org/10.1007/978-981-33-4336-8_12

networked industrial infrastructure and intelligent production systems, the industrial production efficiency is greatly improved. In IIoT paradigm, industrial intelligent control system is an important part, which can support intelligent industrial production with the abilities of autonomous decision-making and system autonomy [2].

Currently, industrial production presents new trends such as processes upstream and downstream coupling, complex and changeable objects, network coordination, and multiple sources of information. Due to limited computing and storage resources, traditional PLC and DCS control stations cannot cope with the control requirements of complex production processes with nonlinear, time-varying, and distributed parameters. Moreover, it cannot meet the urgent needs of smart factory applications for intelligent perception, autonomous decision-making and network collaboration functions. Therefore, it has become a new development trend of that enable industrial control systems to have intelligent control capabilities with cloud-side collaboration, and achieve real-time perception, real-time control and intelligent analysis close to the industrial field.

In our previous works, we have proposed the principle and system architecture of software-defined edge computing (SDEC) to realize the unified management, reconstruction, sharing, reuse and collaboration of edge device resources [3]. In this paper, combined with the ideas and technologies of SDEC and CPS, we propose the edge computing-based solution and framework of software-defined industrial intelligent control (SDIIC) for the autonomous and intelligent control of industry. It mainly consists of SDEC platform at the software level and software-defined edge controller at the hardware level. The SDEC platform uses techniques such as semantic modeling and knowledge graphs to virtualize, abstract, and digitize hardware devices on the edge. The control and management functions of devices are separated from hardware. Combining device resource scheduling and orchestration, sharing coordination, rule engine and other service capabilities, the edge hardware resources of industrial control system can realize flexible management and autonomous coordination in the way of software.

The scheme and system architecture of software-defined edge controller is designed by adopting a multi-processor hybrid heterogeneous hardware framework. It adopts lightweight virtualization technology to realize the virtualized mapping, scheduling, orchestration and management of hardware resources in the controller, and realizes optimal scheduling and dynamic reconstruction of computing capability in a manner of software definition. It can implement software-defined virtual controllers with differentiated control and computing capabilities on common standardized hardware resources. Software-defined edge controller can simultaneously support real-time task processing such as logic control, process control, and motion control, as well as non-real-time task processing such as industrial vision, deep learning, and intelligent optimization. The hardware requirements of edge intelligent control are met.

The target of SDIIC is to enable the intelligent control, intelligent computing, autonomous collaboration and system autonomy in the edge side. Based on the SDEC platform and software-defined edge controller, software and hardware integrated industrial intelligent control solutions with software definition as the core can be realized to support the development of IIoT.

The remainder of this paper is organized as follows. Section 2 introduces the evolution direction of IIoT architecture from the vertical perspective and horizontal perspective.

Section 3 proposes the system architecture of SDIIC. Section 4 proposes the industrial intelligent control oriented SDEC platform scheme. Section 5 proposes the scheme and system architecture of software-defined edge controller. Section 6 draws a conclusion.

2 The Evolution Direction of IIoT Architecture

2.1 Vertical Perspective

As shown in Fig. 1, we compare the current and future IIoT architecture from the vertical perspective. It is mainly reflected in the following aspects:

- The currently closed and chimney-style application development mode will gradually move towards openness, sharing and collaboration.
- The industrial assets such as hardware resources, data, information, knowledge, and service capabilities are shared and reused by various industrial applications through edge computing platform and cloud platform.
- The upper-layer applications are decoupled from the lower-layer hardware, and application developers do not need to care about the deployment details of the lower-layer hardware [4, 5].
- The underlying devices can be freely combined, flexibly arranged, and deployed on demand based on application requirements like "building blocks" [6].
- The binding hardware-defined mode, which industrial applications and hardware resources are tightly coupled, will gradually transform into a new flexible and programmable software-defined mode [7, 8].

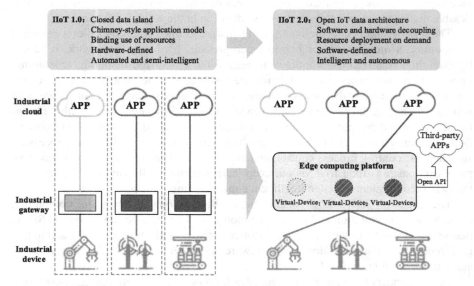

Fig. 1. Vertical comparison of current and future IIoT architecture.

2.2 Horizontal Perspective

We compare the current and future IIoT architecture from the horizontal perspective in Fig. 2. For the traditional five-layer architecture based on ISA-95 standard, although each system has a clear division of labor and is relatively independent, there are still some problems to be solved. For example, data and information island, complex interfaces, data delays, difficulties in data fusion, system lock-in, and lack of interoperability standards. Moreover, most of the industrial control system infrastructure in this architecture mode is based on dedicated hardware, which limits the flexibility of system.

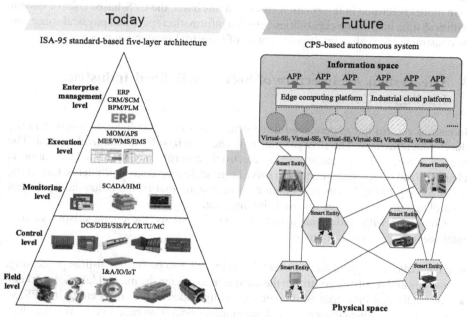

Fig. 2. Horizontal comparison of current and future IIoT architecture.

In the future, the smart entity will be the basic component of new IIoT architecture. The smart entity is a system unit with decision-making ability. It includes not only intelligent industrial equipment, but also the end-to-end system composed of computing power, algorithms and terminal devices. The most significant feature of smart entity is the ability to make independent decisions, which can realize end-to-end closed-loop control applications. Multiple smart entities can also realize interconnection and mutual collaboration to implement complex intelligent industrial applications.

The future IIoT will develop in the direction of the autonomous system based on CPS. The autonomy is reflected in two levels.

- Smart entity level: the smart entity itself can make independent decisions and implement some simple and low-latency intelligent control applications.

- Edge computing platform and cloud platform level: through the model of "Platform + APPs", more complex and intelligent industrial applications can be implemented by combining with these technologies and capabilities such as intelligent analysis, multi-source data integration, resource optimization scheduling, and multiple smart entities collaboration.

In the CPS-based autonomous system, on the one hand, smart entities can achieve interconnection, intercommunication, and interoperability through new industrial network technologies (e.g., OPC UA, TSN, 5G, etc.). On the other hand, through digitally modeling the smart device objects in physical space, a one-to-one corresponding digital twin model is formed in information space. On this basis, the CPS-based control system with real-time interaction capabilities between information space and physical space can be constructed to realize intelligent control of industrial production process [9].

3   The System Architecture of Software-Defined Industrial Intelligent Control

Industrial control has experienced three generations of technological evolution in the development history. The first generation is characterized by mechanical control. The second generation is characterized by electronic control. And the third generation is characterized by computer control to solve large-scale loop control problems. Currently, it is evolving to the fourth-generation control system, that is, the industrial intelligent control system, whose core feature is intelligence.

Compared with traditional industrial control systems, the characteristics of new intelligent control are as follows:

- It can collect various data from the edge side, and also perform real-time processing, analysis and feedback control in the edge side to reduce the manual labor of workers.
- The traditional industrial equipment can be upgraded to the smart entity in CPS, so that it has the self-management and autonomous operation capabilities with the characteristics of self-awareness, self-adaptation, autonomous control and self-diagnosis.
- It has the capabilities of edge data collection, edge data processing, edge AI inference and decision-making, real-time control, intelligent coordination among various devices, and edge security.
- The computing capability of controller hardware is stronger. And it can be flexibly defined and combined with software for different application scenarios to provide flexible control capabilities.
- Through the cloud-edge collaboration mechanism, the powerful processing capabilities of cloud can be introduced into control system to support complex and diverse industrial applications [10].

As shown in Fig. 3, we propose a system architecture of SDIIC. On the whole, it is an "end-edge-cloud" collaborative architecture. The cloud computing-based industrial internet platform provides intelligent management, industrial intelligence, and big data services for production and operation, and enables intelligent control at the edge. The controller layer includes both software-defined edge controller and traditional PLC/DCS. And software-defined edge controller can be used as edge computing node of traditional PLC/DCS to provide stronger computing capability support. Edge computing platforms are deployed on edge servers, industrial computers and other hardware with strong computing capability to provide information modelling, basic edge services, edge intelligence, cloud-edge collaboration and other capabilities in edge-side.

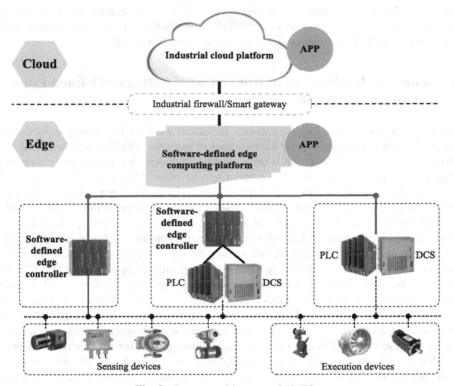

Fig. 3. System architecture of SDIIC.

For the proposed SDIIC solution, it mainly consists of the following two key technologies in both software and hardware.

- Software level: software-defined edge computing platform. By digitizing, virtualizing, and abstracting the description and modeling of industrial edge hardware devices, the virtual device twin model is formed. The basic capabilities and services of software-defined edge computing platform are constructed to realize the unified management and control, sharing and intelligent collaboration of edge device resources. An edge-side industrial autonomous system is also formed.
- Hardware level: software-defined edge controller. The edge controller adopts multi-processor hybrid heterogeneous architecture. Using lightweight virtualization technology, the hardware resources (such as computing, storage, network, and IO) in the

edge controller are virtualized, scheduled, orchestrated and managed. So the optimal scheduling and dynamic reconstruction of computing capacities are implemented in a software-defined manner. The software-defined virtual controllers have differentiated control and computing capability, and can support both real-time and non-real-time task processing simultaneously to realize industrial intelligent control at the edge.

Relying on the software-defined edge computing platform and the software-defined edge controller, the capabilities of intelligent control, intelligent computing, autonomous coordination and system autonomy are implemented at edge-side. And the software and hardware integrated intelligent control system solution is realized.

4   Industrial Intelligent Control Oriented Software-Defined Edge Computing Platform Scheme

The SDEC is based on the ideas of software definition and CPS. From the perspective of cyber-physical space mapping, the technologies of software definition and virtualization modeling are extended to edge hardware resources (including: terminal device resources, edge control device resources, edge computing resources, edge storage resources) and edge application services. The goal of SDEC is to build an intelligent edge autonomous system to realize intelligent control and closed-loop applications in the edge side [11].

According to the characteristics of SDEC technologies and IIoT applications, we propose the SDEC platform for industrial intelligent control, as shown in Fig. 4. The device resources in the edge side include sensing devices, execution devices, smart entity devices, controllers, edge computing nodes, and edge storage devices. The SDEC solution describes and models these device resources in a digitized, virtualized, and abstract manner. The virtual device twin models are constructed and used as the cornerstone and base of IIoT applications. In SDEC platform, some basic functions and capabilities are implemented, including edge device resource scheduling and orchestration, virtual controller orchestration, lightweight rule engine, lightweight AI inference engine adapted to edge-side, knowledge base/rule library/component library/basic algorithm library, container management/microservice, etc. It realizes unified management and control, sharing and intelligent collaboration of edge-side device resources, and supports edge intelligent applications such as motion control, logic control, equipment fault diagnosis, and industrial machine vision. This solution can realize system autonomy on the industrial edge side, and enable the edge hardware resources of industrial control system to realize flexible management and autonomous coordination in software.

In IIoT application solution based on SDEC platform, on the one hand, the edge hardware devices are abstracted and modeled into virtual device twin models. There is a one-to-one correspondence between physical device and digital twin model [12]. They can synchronize with each other through real-time dynamic interaction. Physical device can synchronize the status and data to digital twin model in real time for platform and application to make decision. At the same time, the digital twin model can also synchronize the decision results of platform and application to physical device to execute decision instructions. To this end, the intelligent industrial control in edge side and the cyber-physical space integration and interaction are realized. On the other hand, the

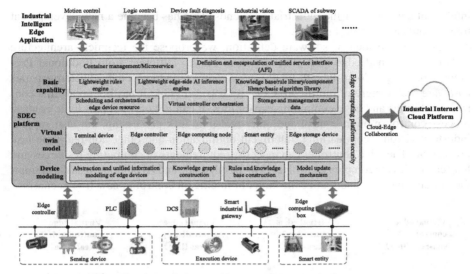

Fig. 4. Technical architecture of SDEC platform.

control, management, and scheduling functions of devices are decoupled and separated from hardware and implemented in software. Through the on-demand configuration and dynamic reorganization of virtualized resources, the sharing and reuse of edge hardware resources can be realized. At the same time, the collaboration mechanism, linkage mechanism and control logic between physical devices become editable and executable in the form of knowledge base and rule library. Combined with the basic capabilities of rule engine and inference engine, intelligent collaboration and system autonomy in edge side can be implemented. Through the unified interface (API) definition and encapsulation of device twin model, knowledge and rule base, edge basic services and capabilities, the upper-level applications can easily call various models, data and basic services without paying too much attention to the deployment details of the underlying hardware devices. This reduces the amount of code development and simplifies application development and deployment.

The SDEC platform can connect into the industrial cloud platform to collaborate with the remote industrial cloud services. Depending on the capabilities of cloud-based big data training, multi-source data fusion analysis, global management and control, cloud-edge collaboration-based intelligent production line control and optimization can be implemented.

5   Software-Defined Edge Controller Scheme

In smart factory, there are some new features and requirements, e.g., multi-type intelligent equipment, multi-machine dynamic cooperative control, networked cooperative manufacturing. It is urgent to research the edge controller with cloud-edge cooperation and intelligent control abilities to realize real-time perception, real-time control and intelligent analysis near the industrial field ends. This has become a new development trend of industrial control system.

Based on the idea of software definition, we propose the technical architecture of software-defined edge controller shown in Fig. 5. Different from traditional Programmable Logic Controller (PLC), the edge controller adopts a hybrid heterogeneous hardware architecture of multi-core CPU + GPU + FPGA. It has both real-time control capabilities and edge computing capabilities. It can not only support logic control, process control, motion control and other real-time task processing, but also support industrial vision, deep learning, intelligent optimization and other non-real-time task processing. The edge controller can meet the requirements of computing resources and load capacities for complex control tasks in the edge side and AI computing tasks in smart factory applications, and realize the target of intelligent control in new IIoT scenarios.

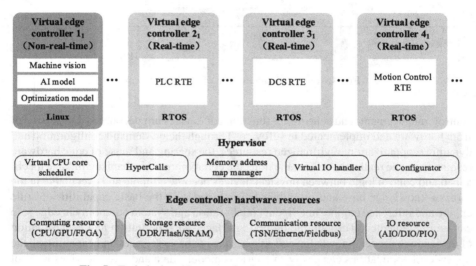

Fig. 5. Technical architecture of software-defined edge controller.

1) Edge controller hardware resources

The hardware resources of edge controller include computing resource, storage resource, communication resource and IO resource. There are different types of computing resource. CPU is responsible for supporting high-speed closed loop control. GPU is responsible for supporting machine vision, AI model and optimization model inference. And CPU + FPGA is responsible for supporting high-speed and high-precision motion control. The storage resource consists of DDR, flash, SRAM, etc. The communication resource consists of TSN, Ethernet, fieldbus, etc. The IO resource consists of AIO, DIO, and PIO. All these resources form the hardware foundation of software-defined edge controller.

2) Resource virtualization (Hypervisor)

Hypervisor is responsible for managing the resource allocation and virtualization of each virtual edge controller. It includes the following key technologies.

- Virtual CPU core scheduler: The instruction sequence of virtual CPU inside each virtual controller is allocated to the actual physical CPU to run according to the scheduling strategy.
- HyperCalls: It is responsible for providing the external interface of the hypervisor layer, and resource management interface calls for the virtual device driver layer and Root OS.
- Memory address map manager: Each virtual controller runs in the virtual machine's physical address space pre-allocated by the hypervisor layer, and only has access rights to this address space. Each virtual controller runs and accesses space is isolated from each other. The memory address map manager is responsible for converting the physical address of virtual controller into the actual machine physical address.
- Virtual IO handler: It is responsible for processing the IO request of each virtual controller and routing it to the physical IO driver to complete the real IO operation.
- Configurator: It supports the configuration of virtual resources occupied by each virtual controller. The module establishes the actual mapping relationship between virtual resources (e.g., virtual CPU, virtual device, virtual memory) and physical resources (e.g., physical CPU, physical device, physical memory) occupied by each virtual controller according to the configuration.

The operating system in virtual edge controller includes two types: Guest OS and Root OS.

- Guest OS: In addition to the conventional functions of traditional OS, it also includes a virtual peripheral driver program, which completes the operation function of the virtual peripheral through the HyperCalls module.
- Root OS: Hypervisor is responsible for managing each virtual edge controller. The processing of this module must be streamlined, otherwise the execution efficiency will be greatly reduced. Therefore, Hypervisor is responsible for processing the key tasks with a short execution time, and the tasks that take a long time are handled by Root OS. Root OS adds a new virtualization component based on the original local OS function. The component is responsible for the auxiliary execution of each task request from virtual machine.

3) Virtual edge controller

The above virtualization method performs virtual mapping, scheduling, orchestration and management of hardware resources in edge controller, and realizes network-based computing power optimal scheduling and dynamic reconstruction in a software-defined way. The diversified virtual controllers with different control and computing capabilities are constructed for meeting different application requirements.

In the software-defined edge controller, a physical controller can virtualize multiple real-time systems and multiple non-real-time systems. They can support real-time control and edge intelligent computing tasks at the same time, and realize the collaboration between multiple industrial control subsystems. For example, on a production line, an edge controller can control multiple six-axis industrial robots and two-axis positioner systems at the same time. With the assistance of industrial vision, they can perform production tasks collaboratively while completing image-based product defect detection.

The edge controller can interconnect and intercommunicate with the industrial cloud platform, and send the industrial data collected from the edge side to the cloud platform for big data analysis and AI model training. The cloud platform sends the trained model to the edge controller to perform model inference at the edge side. This scheme can realize intelligent control of cloud-edge collaboration.

The software-defined edge controller solution integrates real-time and non-real-time control systems such as industrial control, edge computing, and industrial vision. It opens up the platform capabilities of edge and cloud. It has the characteristics of integration, intelligence, real-time, and flexible expansion. This provides a new solution with high-efficiency, differentiation, low cost, space saving, and easy maintenance for networked intelligent manufacturing.

6   Conclusion

This paper has proposed the solution and framework of SDIIC to realize the goal of industrial intelligent control based on edge computing from two levels of software and hardware. For the level of software, the SDEC platform scheme has been proposed. The flexible management and autonomous collaboration of edge devices are realized by software-defined modeling to support real-time industrial applications. For the level of hardware, the system architecture and scheme of software-defined edge controller have been proposed. By virtualizing the hardware resources in edge controller, the optimal scheduling and dynamic reconfiguration of controller resources are realized. It can provide differentiated service capabilities, and build software-defined virtual controller that can support both real-time and non-real-time task processing to meet the different hardware requirements of industrial intelligent control. The proposed SDIIC scheme aims at building an intelligent industrial control system. It uses software to define the hardware, and strives to provide flexible and efficient edge intelligent control services. This solution can be applied to discrete industry, process industry, smart rail transit, smart subway and other industrial fields, and promote the intelligent development of IIoT.

Acknowledgements. This work was supported by the National Key R&D Program of China (No.2019YFB1705100).

References

1. Xu, H., Yu, W., Griffith, D., Golmie, N.: A survey on industrial internet of things: a cyber-physical systems perspective. IEEE Access **6**, 78238–78259 (2018)

2. Choo, K.R., Gritzalis, S., Park, J.H.: Cryptographic solutions for industrial Internet-of-Things: research challenges and opportunities. IEEE Trans. Industr. Inf. **14**(8), 3567–3569 (2018)
3. Hu, P., Chen W.: Software-defined edge computing (SDEC): principles, open system architecture and challenges. In: 2019 IEEE SmartWorld, Ubiquitous Intelligence & Computing, Advanced & Trusted Computing, Scalable Computing & Communications, Cloud & Big Data Computing, Internet of People and Smart City Innovation (Smart-World/SCALCOM/UIC/ATC/CBDCom/IOP/SCI), pp. 8–16. IEEE (2019)
4. Hu, P., Ning, H., Chen, L., Daneshmand, M.: An open Internet of Things system architecture based on software-defined device. IEEE Internet Things J. **6**(2), 2583–2592 (2019)
5. Kreutz, D., Ramos, F.M.V., Veríssimo, P.E., Rothenberg, C.E., Azodolmolky, S., Uhlig, S.: Software-defined networking: a comprehensive survey. Proc. IEEE **103**(1), 14–76 (2015)
6. Mei, H.: Understanding "software-defined" from an OS perspective: technical challenges and research issues. Sci. China (Inf. Sci.) **60**, 271–273 (2017). https://doi.org/10.1007/s11432-017-9240
7. Wan, J., Tang, S., Shu, Z., Di, L., Vasilakos, A.V.: Software-defined industrial Internet of Things in the context of industry 4.0. IEEE Sens. J. **16**(20), 7373–7380 (2016)
8. Hu, P.: A system architecture for software-defined industrial Internet of Things. In: IEEE International Conference on Ubiquitous Wireless Broadband (ICUWB). IEEE (2015)
9. Darabseh, A., Freris, N.M.: A software-defined architecture for control of IoT cyberphysical systems. Cluster Comput. **22**(4), 1107–1122 (2019). https://doi.org/10.1007/s10586-018-02889-8
10. Kaur, K., Garg, S., Aujla, G.S., Kumar, N., Rodrigues, J.J.P.C., Guizani, M.: Edge computing in the industrial Internet of Things environment: software-defined-networks-based edge-cloud interplay. IEEE Commun. Mag. **56**(2), 44–51 (2018)
11. Hu, P., Chen, W., He, C., Li, Y., Ning, H.: Software-defined edge computing (SDEC): principle, open IoT system architecture, applications, and challenges. IEEE Internet Things J. **7**(7), 5934–5945 (2020)
12. Walter, T., Parreiras, F.S., Staab, S.: An ontology-based framework for domain-specific modeling. Softw. Syst. Model. **13**(1), 83–108 (2012). https://doi.org/10.1007/s10270-012-0249-9

Wi-Sector - A Novel Sector-Based WiFi Scheduling

Jie Yang⑩, Li Feng$^{(\boxtimes)}$ ⑩, Hong Liang⑩, Tong Jin⑩, and Fangxin Xu⑩

Macau University of Science and Technology, Taipa, Macau
jiejiedeyouxiang@163.com, lfeng@must.edu.mo, coolboom@126.com,
JinTongMindy@163.com, fzxy002763@gmail.com

Abstract. In dense WiFi networks, transmission collisions become more and more serious. Conventional mechanisms only have limited performance improvement. In this paper, we borrow the hard-disk sector idea to sectorize the whole coverage of a dense network and hence propose a Wi-Fi sector (Wi-Sector) design to solve the collision problem fundamentally. With Wi-Sector, the access point (AP) first silences all nodes, and then activates each sector sequentially. Because each sector only includes a small number node, Wi-Sector can greatly reduce the contention collision and significantly improve the system throughput of dense networks. Extensive simulations verify that our Wi-Sector design is very effective.

Keywords: WiFi · Dense network · Collision · Sectorization

1 Introduction

In recent years, with the growing popularity of Internet of Things (IoT), Wi-Fi network devices have increased exponentially. This makes wireless channel congestion, transmission collision, and hidden/exposed terminal problem more and more serious.

Usually, there are two methods to solve these problems in large-scale WiFi dense networks. One is the contention-window (CW)-based adjustment method. In this method, before data transmission, a node chooses a random backoff count between 0 and CW. The node decreases its backoff counter by 1 if the channel is sensed idle and suspends its backoff counter otherwise. When the backoff count is decreased to 0, the node transmits its data. In case that this transmission experiences a collision, the node doubles its CW. However, this method has the following drawbacks: 1. a large population of nodes mean a long CW, which will lead to much time waste in channel contention, 2. the optimal CW requires the knowledge on the number n of nodes, which is often difficult to obtain. Another is the request-to-send/clear-to-send (RTS/CTS) method. In this method, before sending a data frame, a node sends a RTS frame to reserve the channel. If it receives a CTS feedback, the channel reservation succeeds and therefore it can transmit data successfully. Otherwise, it will experience a RTS collision. In 802.11, the headers of data and RTS/CTS are transmitted at a basic rate, and the payloads of data and RTS/CTS are transmitted at a data rate. When the data rate is small so that the whole data transmission time is far larger than the RTS transmission time, this method works very well. However,

H. Ning and F. Shi (Eds.): CyberDI 2020/CyberLife 2020, CCIS 1329, pp. 154–162, 2020.
https://doi.org/10.1007/978-981-33-4336-8_13

when the data rate is far larger than the basic rate (say, the data rate = 1 Gbps and the basic rate = 24 Mbps in 802.11ac [1]), both transmission times are almost equal and the method becomes worse because it introduces additional transmission times of RTS and CTS frames before each data transmission. On the other hand, a large population of nodes will also lead to serious RTS collision.

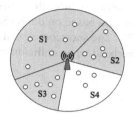

Fig. 1. Software-defined MAC for sector scheduling.

For a large-scale WiFi dense network, the above two methods only have limited performance improvement. In this paper, we borrow the hard-disk sector idea to divide a whole WiFi coverage into multiple sectors, each sector including a small number of nodes; Fig. 1 shows that the network coverage is divided into 4 sectors (S1 to S4). Benefitting the sectorization solution, we can fundamentally solve the collision problem and improve the system performance of dense networks significantly. Our contributions are summarized as follows.

- Propose a Wi-Fi sector (Wi-Sector) design to group contention nodes and perform sector scheduling. With Wi-Sector, the access point (AP) first silences all nodes, and then activates each sector sequentially via directional beam. In this way, we can reduce contention collision and improve system throughput of dense networks significantly.
- Run extensive simulations that verify that our Wi-Sector design is very effective and can significantly outperform conventional methods in terms of throughput.

The rest of the paper is organized as follows. Section 2 summarizes related works. Section 3 proposes the Wi-Sector design. Section 4 evaluates the system performance of WiFi-Sector. And finally, Sect. 5 concludes this paper.

2 Relate Works

Currently, there are mainly two types of methods that focus on solving the collision problem under large-scale networks [2–6]: Dynamic CW adjustment and RTS/CTS-based methods. These two methods and their shortcomings are briefly described below.

Dynamic CW Adjustment Method: This method reduces transmission collision via contention window adjustment. [2] use the channel observation-based mechanism to monitor the real-time collision probability of the channel and implement dynamic adjustment of the contention window accordingly, avoiding the high delay caused by blindly multiplying the contention window. [3] comprehensively consider the channel BER adjustment algorithm to design the contention window under the dense network to obtain higher performance. [4] introduce the reinforcement learning method to observe the channel state, and select the optimal contention window accordingly. However, these methods only consider optimizing network performance by adjusting the contention window. In a dense environment, the backoff overhead is relatively large.

RTS/CTS-Based Methods: This method reduces the collision via RTS/CTS-based channel reservation. [5, 6] are an extension based on the RTS/CTS model, but in RTS/CTS, each transmission requires an RTS. The shortcomings of the/CTS handshake still exist, resulting in additional control overhead when collision resolution.

3   Proposed Wi-Sector

3.1   PHY Design

Here, we present the hardware of the AP that supports multiple antennas for directional beamforming. Based on hardware support, our design can improve the 802.11ac version or newer routing protocols, as shown in Fig. 2. 802.11ac routing already supports using up to 8 antennas in a single channel to form beams, so it can be able to provide directional beams. In our design, we also assume that AP has up to 8 antennas, so that it can perform beamforming under a single channel, and these antennas are all omnidirectional antennas. In particular, these 8 antennas can provide beamforming technology in the form of digital precoding in accordance according to 802.11 protocol standard to achieve directional scanning.

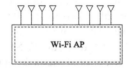

Fig. 2. A design of Wi-Sector AP.

3.2   MAC Frames

Conventional WiFi have three types of WiFi frames: management, control and data frames. Here, we present theirs setting for silencing/activating nodes in Wi-Sector.

In the design of Wi-Sector, NAV parameters are set based on the Duration/AID parameter area. In order to implement the sector-based time-sharing contention strategy, we need to control the Duration/AID field in the AP/STA sent frame. In 802.11 standard, the Duration/AID field has two different functions. As shown in Fig. 3, if the highest bit is set to 0, it is used as the Duration parameter, and the node will receive this parameter and update it to the node's own NAV timer; differently, if the highest bit is set to 1, then this parameter is used as an AID parameter, and the node will not update this parameter to its NAV timer.

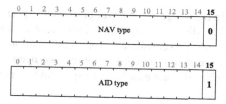

Fig. 3. Duration/AID field in 802.11 frame

Therefore, in this design, due to the reason that we need to use APs for global scheduling, we use different types of Duration/AID field to set mechanisms for frames of different objects.

- Frames sent by AP:

  - Management frame: The Duration/AID fields are all set as the Duration parameter for purpose of implementing partition scheduling.
  - Control Frame/Data frame: Control frame includes ACK and other different frames, and the data frame can be downlink data. Here, the AP sets the Duration/AID field in these frames as the AID parameter.

- Frames sent by STA: Since nodes are scheduled object, the Duration/AID parameters of the management frame, control frame, and data frame sent by the node should be set to AID.

3.3 MAC Protocol

The basic idea of Wi-Sector is to divide sectors into time-sharing access, i.e., only allowing nodes in a sector to contend channel each time. This method restricts the number of nodes for channel access and therefore reduces collision probability. The MAC layer protocol of Wi-Sector contains 3 stages: topology generation, sector generation and channel access. With the help of Fig. 4, we present the above three stages.

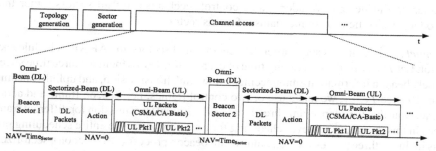

Fig. 4. MAC protocol overview.

Topology Generation: In this stage, the AP will periodically perform background scans to obtain information, i.e., direction angle and basic service set identifiers (BSSID), about surrounding nodes, so as to calculate the physical location of each node and form a physical topology. To generate the entire topology, we need to obtain basic service set identifier (BSSID) of each node and its corresponding direction of arrival (DOA) through the scans.

- Obtaining BSSID: In our design, the AP and nodes works in CSMA/CA basic mode and the AP acquires BSSIDs of nodes by scanning background flows in real time during the omni-beam up-link (UL) process. During the scanning, the AP will first extract BSSID field from the MAC header of a node's frame in the flows, and then cache the BSSID to a database.
- Obtaining DOA: The AP can estimate DOAs using information extracted from physical headers of frames during the scanning of background flows, since nodes adopt multi-antenna mechanism. This mechanism has been adopted by many wireless related technologies, e.g., [7, 8].

Sector Generation: In this stage, after obtaining the physical topology, the AP will divide the network into several sectors according to a preset restricted number of nodes (i.e., N_{sector_node}) and the topology information. This sectorization method makes it able for the AP to later schedule each sector via directional beamforming. To ensure the network performance of each sector, we set the maximum number of nodes in each Sector to N_{sector_node}. As shown in Fig. 1, we obtain partitions via the control of arc and set the number of nodes in each sector to a fixed constant value. If the distribution of nodes in a sector is looser, the arc of the sector will be larger and if the distribution of nodes tighter, the arc is smaller.

In addition, our sector partition uses an incremental partition strategy, which can be divided into the following two steps: Step1). Divide the total number of nodes N_{Total} by N_{sector_node}, and then add 1 to the integer part of the result (i.e., dealing the result through a ceiling function). The integer part of result represents a saturated number of nodes in a sector, which is equal to N_{sector_node}. Step2). Let the remainder of N_{Total} divided by N_{sector_node} be the number of nodes for the last sector. Since the number of nodes in this sector is less than those of other sectors, the throughput of this sector will be slightly smaller. In our design, we adopt same control mechanism for all sectors rather than introduce a specific control mechanism for this sector.

Channel Access: In this stage, after the generation of sectors, the AP will schedule each sector. Let T_{Sector} be the scheduling time of each sector. T_{Sector} includes three time slices, namely beacon information announcement, downlink transmission, and uplink transmission. To slice T_{Sector}, we make use of two control frames, i.e., beacon frame and action frame. Note that we adopt omni-directional or directional transmission for different frame types in this design, to achieve scheduling for a specific area. The entire scheduling process includes three processes, i.e., omni-beam beacon process (OB-Beacon), sectorized-beam downlink process (SB-DL), omni-beam uplink process (OB-UL). Below, we detail each process.

- Omni-beam beacon process (OB-Beacon)

At the beginning of each sector switching process, the AP will use omni-directional transmission (omni-beam) to send beacon frames, as shown in Fig. 4. Here, a beacon frame contains the following two fields: 1). Duration, which silences all nodes by setting them to NAV state; 2). AP clock, i.e., timing synchronization function, with which nodes will perform time synchronization with the AP.

- Sectorized-beam downlink process (SB-DL)

After the transmission of beacon frames, the AP executes downlink transmission process. At this time, since all nodes are set to NAV state, the AP can immediately send a downlink data frame to a node in an activated sector following beacon frames via directional transmission, after a SIFS interval. After the node receives the data frame, it needs to send a ACK feedback. In our design, we require that the duration field in the data/ACK frames to be set to AID type, so that the frames will not affect the sectors working mode in the NAV state. After a fixed time duration of the entire SB-DL downlink process, the AP will send an action control frame (which contains similar information as a beacon frame) to end the SB-DL process via directional transmission, and activate the uplink transmission opportunities for the nodes in this activated sector. The control frame is transmitted using directional beamforming, and the duration field in the frame is set to NAV = 0.

- Omni-beam uplink process (OB-UL)

After completion of downlink transmission, the AP will send a control frame to explicitly activate nodes in a sector. Note that all nodes can be controlled no matter whether they are associated with the AP since we adopt virtual carrier sensing mechanism of NAV technology. Then all nodes in this sector can perform channel contention via uplink transmission. The process of uplink transmission follows the standard CSMA/CA protocol.

Following the above-mentioned processes of channel access, the AP sequentially schedules each sector, so that the whole network can operate according to the designed protocol we propose.

4 Simulation

In this section, we discuss the performance of Wi-Sector. We use MatLab to simulate the Wi-Sector protocol, and the single simulation time is 100 s. We assume that there are at most 100 nodes in the network area covered by an AP. All nodes are partitioned according to a fixed number of nodes (i.e., N_{sector_node}). As the number of nodes continues to increase, the number of partitions should increase accordingly. Since we are mainly concerned with the upstream traffic of the node, we assume that the downstream traffic of the AP is 0. The detailed simulation parameters are shown in Table 1.

Figure 5 plots the system throughput via the total number of nodes. Its x-axis denotes the total number of nodes, ranging from 1 to 100, and Its y-axis denotes the throughput

Table 1. Simulation settings.

N_{Total}	100	R_{Basic}	12 Mbps
N_{sector_node}	10	L_{RTS}	20 Bytes
T_{Sector}	32768 us	L_{CTS}	14 Bytes
T_{PHY_Header}	20 us	L_{ACK}	14 Bytes
R_{ext}	54 Mbps	L_{Beacon}	124 Bytes
L_{MPDU}	1528 Bytes	L_{Action}	124 Bytes
T_{SIFS}	16 us	T_{SLOT}	9 us

in Mbps. In the figure, the black dotted line is the throughput in CSMA/CA-Basic mode, the blue dotted line is the throughput in CSMA/CA-RTS/CTS mode, and the red dotted line is the throughput corresponding to the Wi-Sector proposed in this article.

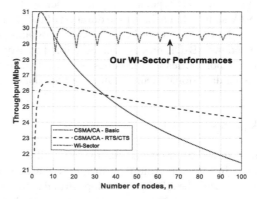

Fig. 5. Throughput performance (Color figure online)

From a holistic perspective, we can see that the throughput of Wi-Sector is significantly better than CSMA/CA-Basic mode and CSMA/CA-RTS/CTS mode. From this figure, we have the following observations.

- As the number of nodes increases (within 5 nodes), the throughput of the three methods all increase. This is because the increase in the number of nodes will lead to the increase in the transmission probability of the node, and at the meantime the collision probability still maintains a small value, so it will not have a major impact on the throughput.
- When the number of nodes is between 5 and 100, the throughput of CSMA/CA-Basic drops sharply as the number of nodes increases, while the throughput of CSMA/CA-RTS/CTS decreases slowly as the number of nodes increases. The throughput of Wi-Sector is almost the same as the number of nodes increases (in fact, it decreases slowly). This is because we control the network through sector partition scheduling, so that collisions among large-scale nodes contention caused by simultaneous contention

can be avoided. We set up to 10 nodes for each ector. If the total number of nodes exceeds 10, we need to divide them.

- In the figure, we can also see that with about 10 nodes for each sector (namely N_{sector_node}), the Wi-Sector's throughput will suddenly drop once, and then gradually rise again. This is because we adopt an incremental partitioning strategy. For example, when there are 21 nodes, we will divide all nodes into 3 Sectors, which are 2 sectors with fixed 10 nodes, and a sector with 1 node. In channel access process, time-sharing access is performed in accordance with 3 sectors, which will result in a decrease in the throughput of the sector with only one node, and finally weighted to a decrease in the overall throughput. However, as the number of nodes in this sector increases, its throughput gradually rises. When the number of nodes continues to increase, the throughput will periodically drop due to the newly added sectors.

In summary, it can be seen that the Wi-Sector is significantly better than the traditional protocol, and as the number of nodes increases, the throughput of Wi-Sector will not fluctuate significantly and is relatively stable. It shows that our protocol has good adaptability in large-scale and high-density Wi-Fi networks, which can ensure overall throughput and improve network performance.

5 Conclusion

In order to solve the collision problem in large-scale dense networks, this paper designs a new wireless access protocol called Wi-Sector. Wi-Sector divides all nodes of a dense network into different sectors and performs sector scheduling in two steps: 1) make all nodes silent, 2) activate each sector sequentially via directional beamforming. In this way, Wi-sector can significantly reduce the transmission collision of a dense network. A salient feature of Wi-Sector is that it effectively utilizes (rather than modifies) the virtual carrier sense mechanism of conventional WiFi protocols for sector scheduling and therefore has a good compatibility with conventional WiFi protocols. Extensive simulations show that our design can make a dense network keep a high stable throughput and greatly outperforms related designs.

Acknowledgement. This work is funded in part by the National Natural Science Foundation of China (File no. 61872451 and 61872452), in part by the Science and Technology Development Fund, Macau SAR (File no. 0098/2018/A3, 0076/2019/A2 and 0037/2020/A1).

References

1. IEEE Std 802.11, Part 11: wireless LAN medium access control (MAC) and physical layer (PHY) specifications
2. Shahin, N., Ali, R., Kim, S.W., Kim, Y.-T.: Cognitive backoff mechanism for IEEE802. 11ax high-efficiency WLANs. J. Commun. Netw. **21**(2), 158–167 (2019)
3. Deng, D.-J., Ke, C.-H., Chen, H.-H., Huang, Y.-M.: Contention window optimization for IEEE 802.11 DCF access control. IEEE Trans. Wirel. Commun. **7**(12), 5129–5135 (2008)

4. Ali, R., Shahin, N., Zikria, Y.B., Kim, B.-S., Kim, S.W.: Deep reinforcement learning paradigm for performance optimization of channel observation–based MAC protocols in dense WLANs. IEEE Access **7**, 3500–3511 (2018)

5. Wang, L., Wu, K., Hamdi, M.: Attached-RTS: eliminating an exposed terminal problem in wireless networks. IEEE Trans. Parallel Distrib. Syst. **24**(7), 1289–1299 (2012)

6. Lee, Y.-H., Wu, W.-R.: A WLAN uplink collision-resolving scheme using multi-user beamforming technique. IEEE Trans. Veh. Technol. (2020)

7. Gaber, A., Omar, A.: A Study of wireless indoor positioning based on joint TDOA and DOA estimation using 2-D matrix pencil algorithms and IEEE 802.11ac. IEEE Trans. Wirel. Commun. **14**(5), 2440–2454 (2015)

8. Neri, A., Di Nepi, A., Vegni, A.M.: DOA and TOA based localization services protocol in IEEE 802.11 networks. Wirel. Pers. Commun. **54**(1), 155–168 (2010). https://doi.org/10.1007/s11277-009-9719-y

Author Index

Printed in the United States
By Bookmasters